FIVE CRIES OF YOUTH

Five Cries of Youth

Issues That Trouble Young People Today

Second Revised Edition

Merton P. Strommen
Assisted by Ram Gupta

HarperSanFrancisco
A Division of HarperCollins*Publishers*

Technical Art: Karen L. Klinger/Miller Freeman Graphic Services

FIRST HARPERCOLLINS PAPERBACK EDITION PUBLISHED IN 1993

Library of Congress Cataloging-in-Publication Data

Strommen, Merton P.
  Five cries of youth : issues that trouble young people today /
Merton P. Strommen ; assisted by Ram Gutpa.—2nd rev. ed.
      p.   cm.
  Includes bibliographical references.
  ISBN 0-06-067746-5 (pbk. : alk. paper)
    1. Youth—Conduct of life—Case studies. 2. Youth—Religious
life—Case studies. I. Gupta, Ram. II. Title.
  [BJ1661.S9 1993]
208′.35–dc20   91–59024
                                                                         CIP

---

93 94 95 96 97 RRD(H) 10 9 8 7 6 5 4 3 2 1

This edition is printed on acid-free paper that meets the American
National Standards Institute Z39.48 Standard.

To my sons, Peter, Tim, Jim, John, and David,
who have given me much companionship and joy

The dedication has added meaning in this revised edition. Our fifth
son, David, now serving his Lord in another part of God's Kingdom,
was killed by a bolt of lightning at a youth camp in Colorado, August
12, 1986. He was there as a seminary student, youth director, and
counselor of his own church group.

Contents

Figures

Tables

Acknowledgments

Special acknowledgment, with thanks, is given Dr. Ram Gupta, professor, University of Edmonton, Canada, for his technical assistance. This included not only the trend analysis reported in this updated version but also his assistance, beginning nearly twenty-five years ago, in perfecting the survey instrument.

Thanks also to the many people whose contributions to the original edition have carried over into this one. Here I refer especially to Dorothy Williams for her illustrative characterizations, Nancy Nelson for her poems, and Dr. C. Gilbert Wrenn, my mentor and friend, for his critique of in-process revisions.

A special thanks to my dear wife, Irene, for working with me in bringing rough copies of chapter revisions into final form for publishing. And to sons Jim and John for their initial review of chapter manuscripts.

I gratefully acknowledge also the skilled assistance of Jan Mills, who typed final copy for publication and Dr. Michael J. Donahue, also of Search Institute, who served as critical reviewer.

January, 1988   Merton Strommen

Preface

You may wonder how much change this updated edition of *Five Cries of Youth* shows over its first edition. One naturally assumes that data collected in 1970 no longer describes today's youth, born in the seventies and living their teen years in the eighties.

This version of *Five Cries of Youth* deals with the issue of change in two ways. First, the book presents ten- and fifteen-year trend data illustrating how the dimensions of each cry may or may not have changed by the year 1985. Second, it incorporates research findings from the eighties and nineties. Interestingly these findings corroborate our original data.

The necessity for this revision centers in the fact that ever since its first edition *Five Cries of Youth* has been widely used by people who work with youth in church settings. It has provided a conceptual model that youth ministers have found helpful. Its descriptions of five youth populations (many of which overlap in common characteristics) have alerted youth ministers to the multiple and sometimes contrasting needs of youth being served by the church.

The five cries or preoccupations described in this book identify feelings or emotions that characterize and at times dominate many youth. Underlying each emotion is an unspoken goal cherished by these youth—self-esteem, family love, the welfare of others, a meaningful life, or one's own personal advantage. These implicit goals throw light on the kinds of ministry that will have special meaning and appeal for these youth. The cries to which we refer, with their accompanying emotions and underlying goals, are summarized below.

It may surprise you to find that four of the cries have remained much the same over the past fifteen years; whereas a fifth, the cry of protest, shows significant change. This cry re-

Five Cries—Five Preoccupations

Cry	Emotion	Goal
Self-hatred	Loneliness	Self-esteem
Psychological orphan	Disillusionment	Family love
Protest	Outrage	Welfare of people
Prejudice	Selfishness	Personal advantage
Faith	Joy	Meaningful life

flects the impact of pervasive shifts in our country's value orientation on today's youth.

This phenomenon of little change in four facets of youth's life and a major change in another draws attention to the interplay of psychological and sociological forces. On one hand, the universal concerns of adolescents are like bedrock that remains relatively unchanged over the years. They are only moderately affected by cultural determinants. Our trend analyses confirm the statement I made in the first edition regarding the continuing usefulness of the 1970 data (see page 11). On the other hand, the values, beliefs, and life-styles of church youth show the influence of societal change in their largely muted cry of social concern. The change in their cry, however, is not as great as that seen for American youth in general. It would seem that church youth have been less influenced by the values of the seventies.

Although the "me"-oriented seventies show their eroding effect on youth's life perspective, this pendulumlike shift in youth's values and beliefs may now have reached its furthest point. Signs indicating a swing back in values could usher in a new day of opportunity for youth work in the church.

Trend Analyses

Fortunately we have access to trend data that spans periods of up to twenty years, ending with the year 1985. Such objective data gives us a means of assessing the degree to which change may have occurred for major dimensions in our conceptual model of five cries.

The ideal, of course, would have been to replicate the entire study of 1970. Only those who know how difficult it is to secure funding for such a study, especially where religion is involved, can appreciate why this was not possible. Lacking the ideal, we are summoning evidence from studies that gives us a fair estimate of possible change. To show the development of trends, I have used the years of 1977, 1980, and 1985 as checkpoints. Comparisons can be made at these points, which span periods of from seven to fifteen years.

Our trend information is drawn from two sources, trend studies of American youth in general and trend analyses of church youth. A brief description of these studies is given below, with more precise descriptions given in the chapter notes.

American Youth

A major source of trend information on American youth comes from annual studies of high-school seniors carried out by the University of Michigan. These studies, which began in 1945, sample approximately sixteen thousand seniors each year drawn from randomly selected high schools in the United States. Their survey queries youth on a broad range of topics, including ways of life and values. The resulting description of seniors in American high schools, reported each year in a publication entitled *Monitoring the Future*, can be viewed as information based on "hard data," because the Institute for Social Research, in conducting these surveys, presses for precise samples and valid data. The one flaw of the surveys is that these samples of seniors do not include school dropouts, a significant portion of American youth in that age group. However, these studies do provide important trend data applicable to church youth who generally do graduate from high school.

A second source of information is found in the two national surveys of American youth (1974 and 1983) by the National Association of Secondary School Principals. These surveys probed the ideas, beliefs, and aspirations of America's youth, grades seven to twelve, in public and private schools. One purpose of these surveys was to assess possible differences and similarities between students in the seventies "me generation" and adolescents of the eighties, "the information age." Results of this study were published in *The Mood of American Youth*. This study may be the most comparable to our samples of church youth because it includes students in both junior and senior high school. Furthermore, the national random sample is drawn from both public schools (87 percent) and private schools, 11 percent of those in the sample being church-related schools.

To supplement the above we have used trend data based on a broader spectrum of American youth as reported by Harold Hodgkinson in his 1986 *Education Week Special Report*. He draws on national demographics to chart important trends affecting today's youth and predicting tomorrow's future. His information is based on a broad segment of American youth.

A fourth source is found in the annual surveys of incoming college and university freshmen. Over a twenty-year period random samples drawn annually from among these freshmen give evidence of changes occurring among leadership-type youth. Data from these studies, reported by Alexander Astin in his book *Achieving Academic Excellence*, especially informs our chapter on the cry of social concern.

Another annual survey pertinent to our analysis is a ten-year comparison of the behavior and values of high school achievers during the years 1976 to 85. These achievers are ones randomly selected from the four hundred thousand juniors and seniors listed each year in *Who's Who of American High School Youth*. This information is useful as a trend indicator because these high achievers strongly identify with religious institutions.

Assuming that most young people reflect the values of adult society, we can look at major shifts in adults' values to anticipate changes in youth's values. A 1986 study of trends in America by Oxford Analytica is helpful here. This research firm at Oxford University has carried out over three hundred studies of trends for more than seventy countries and reported its studies of trends in the United States in the book *America in Perspective*

(1986). Parallel to this effort are the trend analyses of Yankelo-vitch, Skelly, and White. This New York research firm monitors fifty-five value trends each year through careful interviewing of a precise random sample of Americans. Though oriented to business, this research firm studies values because it assumes that changes in values signal changes in people's buying habits.

Another useful resource is George Gallup's 1985 publication, *Religion in America,* which reports studies of religion in America over a fifty-year period. Supplementing this report is Gallup's 1986 national study of faith development in persons eighteen years of age and older, *Faith Development and Your Ministry.* His data contributes to the conclusions drawn in chapter 6.

Each of the above sources of trend information supplies what might be termed "hard data" because probability samples are used and care is taken to obtain responses from all persons drawn into the sample.

Church Youth

Over the past twenty-six years Search Institute has main-tained a survey service used by hundreds of congregations and parochial schools. Computers made available by Lutheran Brotherhood of Minneapolis have scored the tens of thousands of answer sheets sent in by youth taking the Youth Research Survey. This survey instrument was the one used by 7,050 high-school youth in 1970 to provide the original data base for this book. Twice we dipped into this data bank of processed answer sheets, once in 1974 and again in 1977, to identify any possible changes in these cries. These we reported in the paperback edi-tion of *Five Cries of Youth.*

Remarkably, scale scores based on our 1977 data are identical on most measures to scores derived from the 1970 data. This fact gives a degree of confidence that the sample of youth using the survey service is a fair representation of church youth, valid at least for charting trends.

In 1980 a solid checkpoint was gained in data collected through a national study of Lutheran youth. This careful study, a census sample of parochial school youth, gave us another indicator of possible change in youth concerns. Our sample of Lutheran youth from 1970 was the basis for making a significant assessment of trends that might have occurred among Lutheran youth by 1980.

In 1984 Search Institute conducted a national survey of 7,551 students randomly selected from the ninth and twelfth grades of 106 Catholic parochial schools serving low-income youth (*Catholic High Schools: Their Impact on Low-Income Students* 1986). These were schools with more than 10 percent enrollment of students whose family income was below the federal poverty line. This sample is especially valuable because it includes a good representation of minorities (black, 1,675; Hispanic, 1,105; Asian, 186; and native American, 163). Four-fifths of these students were Catholic and the rest identified with a variety of denominations. Though this study cannot indicate trends, it does provide another source for evaluating the values, attitudes, and behaviors of church youth in 1984.

In 1987 Dr. Ram Gupta of the University of Edmonton, Canada, added an impressive source of information in his trend analyses of church youth over a period of fifteen years. He compared the original sample of 7,050 church youth from 1970 with 2,200 church youth who took the Youth Research Survey during the years 1983 to 1985.

In this second revision I have added pertinent findings from several studies that reflect the nineties. Two are major studies of Search Institute reported in 1990. The first is *Effective Christian Education: A National Study of Protestant Congregations*. Participating in this study were 11,121 respondents from 561 randomly selected congregations of six Protestant denominations (United Methodist, Presbyterian USA, Evangelical Lutheran Church, Southern Baptist Convention, Disciples of Christ, and United Church of Christ).

The second is *The Troubled Journey: A Profile of American Youth*. It is based on the self-reports of 47,000 students (grades 6–12) found in 111 communities and schools of 25 states.

Introduction

Many parents find that their children's adolescence breeds sleepless nights full with questions. Why has Paul shut us out of his life? Am I too strict? What can I do about the way John is rebelling? Will Jenny ever show interest in a religious faith?

While parents are asking one set of questions, adult leaders in congregations are asking related ones. Are we dealing with a "new breed" in this generation? Does a personal faith make a difference in the lives of American youth? Are the "loyalists" in church youth groups primarily "losers"? Has the pressure cooker of today's living made anxiety a serious issue? Should I take youth's critiques of the church seriously? What can I do about prejudice? What is a healthy religious faith?

This book proposes to apply hard-nosed research to these questions and to indicate directions in which youth ministry ought to go. It is offered in full awareness of the fact that it differs from the conclusions of some highly visible writers on certain youth problems; its claim to authority rests in the previously unavailable research data that has guided my interpretation. These data collected from national samples of church youth have been organized according to highly complex and sophisticated research procedures.

The Focus

In this book you hear the voice of American church youth, who comprise two-thirds of the total population of American young people. These youth, ages fourteen to eighteen, who identify with a United States church body and represent millions of high-school youth, include the dormant and disinterested as well as the vital and active members. In these pages you hear self-reports of their values, beliefs, and opinions and their concerns about themselves, their friends, their world, and their God. If you listen, you can hear cries, rising out of the data with compelling insistence: sobs, angry shouts, hurrahs, protests, and jeers.

The cries that underlie the self-reports of 7,050 representative youth challenge the adequacy of a youth ministry that is all evangelism, all social involvement, all socializing activities, or all doctrinal instruction. They posit five basic needs, or value orientations, requiring five distinct accents in a youth ministry.

The Two Emphases

This book does more than report and summarize the research; it also attempts to catch the significance of youth's cries and point toward ways of responding to them. Beyond objective research facts, it offers an interpretation reflecting my biases and theological stance.

I am doubtful about the claims of those who predict a doleful future for the church. This study and others like it (*A Study of Generations*, 1973, and the *Effective Christian Education Study*, 1990) attest to a vigorous core of committed Christians who reflect in their values, beliefs, and behavior the power of a personal faith. Most church members, youth as well as adults, are hopeful about the future and convinced of the importance of their congregation's mission. This is reflected in the hopeful stance of this book. I believe that one finds in Jesus Christ the alpha and omega of life.

Throughout this book you will find two emphases that are usually strangers. One emphasis is upon rigorous, objective research; the second is upon establishing a rationale for the findings and identifying what is important for the parent and youth leader. It is my hope that this book will encourage a more thoughtful and sustained approach to a home and congregational youth ministry.

It should be understood that this book is not a scientific report but rather the development of a rationale informed by research findings gathered over a period of years and a description of the degree to which change has occurred among church youth.

1. To Hear and Understand the Cries

So runs my dream.
And what am I?
An infant, crying in the night
An infant, crying for the light,
And with no language but a cry?
from "In Memoriam"

Young people, like the rest of us, cry out their needs in many puzzling ways. Some are extremely critical of everyone and everything around them; some plunge into a flurry of service activities or secede from the world by spending every possible moment before the TV. Some turn their backs on friends and family, seeming to shut them out. Others surround themselves with a screen of cheerful insults, jokes, and high-pitched laughter. Still others are caught in a new religious ardor that seems unnatural to their parents.

Because of the indirect ways in which youth speak to us, their cries are often mistaken for something else. But all of them can be expressive of deep human needs that are hard to articulate.

People who sincerely care about young people must not ignore these disguised pleas for direction, help, and understanding, difficult as they are to interpret.

This book is written as an aid to hearing and interpreting the cries. The survey data on which it is based was collected from 7,050 high-school students during the spring and summer of 1970. These were randomly selected from more than a dozen church denominations, from Young Life groups, and from groups with no discernible religious affiliation.

In 1970 student unrest and campus violence were at their peak, not only in colleges throughout the country, but in high schools and even in some junior high schools. The survey data produced a snapshot of church youth's attitudes at a time when dissatisfaction with adult institutions was prevalent among young people. It was an unprecedented time in America's history, frightening to many adults, when the cries of youth were audible and insistent as never before.

One wonders what change twenty-two years have brought to cries rooted in the psyche of youth. For that reason trend data published in 1986 are used in this revision to test the validity of the 1970 information. Furthermore, key findings from several national studies reported in 1990 provide additional reference points as to the relevance of the underlying factors identified in this book. Three of these studies are: *Effective Christian Education: A National Study of Protestant Congregations, The Troubled Journey: A Profile of American Youth,* and *Monitoring the Future* (1988).

Is This Book Necessary?

Until 1970 there was little information on the attitudes, concerns, interests, beliefs, and values of young people who are members of religious institutions. I became aware of this while serving as editor of the comprehensive handbook *Research on Religious Development* (1971). When Havighurst and Keating (coauthors of a chapter in the handbook) combed the material published over four decades, they found little solid research on youth where religion is included as a variable. Of the many chapters set aside for specialized topics and specific age groups, none was as lacking in published research as the chapter on church youth of high-school age.

Now, many years after I have edited this handbook, I find the picture to be the same. Though new studies have probed factors of adolescents' lives, fewer than 2 percent of them have included the religious variable. And most of these studies have assessed religion with only one item (e.g., how often do you attend church or synagogue? or, what is your denominational affiliation?). Three different reviews of research have demonstrated that less than 2 percent of all research studies take the religious dimension seriously (Larson et al., 1983). This is strange in light of the fact that we have been able to demonstrate that some of the best predictors of what people say and do are their values and religious beliefs.[1]

This book is intended to supply facts where before we had only myths, assumptions, and individual experiences to indicate how faith and values interact with adolescent concerns. It supplies a map of territory that those who care about youth must travel. There is no neatly marked route, but landmarks—high ground, swamp, forest, and thicket. With facts in hand we can make more informed choices for the journey.

I have one concern over classifying youth as I do in this book. The danger is that some readers will use the categories to label individuals and then treat them according to that category. Our division into five cries does not imply that a given individual can belong to only one group; he or she may be troubled by both family pressures and low self-esteem. Church youth do not come tidily sectioned off with one problem apiece—which, of course, makes them additionally individual.

One way of handling this problem is to dismiss all attempts to understand the human person in a broad, general way; it is enough to focus on an individual, come to know his uniqueness, and respond accordingly.

Every young person is unique; he has special needs, interests, and potentialities.

But how does one minister to groups of one hundred (or even fifty) young people in a congregation or church-sponsored school? Must there be one hundred different approaches? What about common needs in groups of young people? Is it possible to minister to these categories while recognizing and making allowances for the uniqueness of each person?

Counterculture youth differ from high-school athletes in their values and attitudes toward authority. Young people from tragic home situations contrast with those from happy homes.

Youth must be approached in differing ways because they vary in their views of themselves and life. This does not require stereotyping or labeling, but only sensitivity to the likely meanings of behavioral patterns.

I am not advocating a problem approach to youth. The issue is not, what is John's or Linda's problem? but, what sort of person is John or Linda? How can we help young people find their potential and the fullest enjoyment of life? Our task is to collaborate with young people in discovering ways to solve their problems.

To understand youth's cries is to know where to begin. Solutions emerge in an atmosphere of mutuality (the warmth and interaction of accepting persons) and in the challenge of collaborative activities that lead to a sense of mission in life.

This brings me to what I hope you gain through reading this book. First, I hope you will hear with greater clarity the individual cries implicit in the behavior of young people. The ability to hear does not come quickly and naturally. It is a sensitivity one must learn, as a musician learns to distinguish instruments in a symphony or orchestra, or as an auto mechanic becomes sensitive to the healthy and unhealthy sounds produced by running engines.

Second, I hope you will increase your understanding of what you hear by developing a framework of meaning. If you awaken at night and hear the front door open and close, it is your background of knowledge that causes you to leap to your feet or simply go back to sleep. Is everyone at home and in bed? Is one member still out? The understanding with which you hear the cries of youth gives meaning to what you hear and can help you determine which cries deserve the first attention.

How Do You Make Sense of the Data?

How was it possible to listen to thousands of descriptions of concerns, values, attitudes, beliefs, and behavior and make sense out of that flood of communication? Search Institute's survey has 420 items, developed over a twelve-year period of use and selected for their success in outlining the significant and troublesome areas of a young person's life. In response the young people gave us three million bits of information—an enormous jigsaw puzzle whose cover picture was missing.

Running through the responses we found over twenty-five common threads or characteristics. One characteristic cluster of items centered on family unity, another on personal faults, and a third on youth's concern over national issues, and so on. Listed below are these twenty-five clusters or characteristics by which youth describe themselves and sketch their profiles.[2]

Concerns

1. *Family unity.* Concern over an apparent lack of love and oneness in the family.
2. *Parental understanding.* Feelings about a lack of understanding and acceptance between youth and parents.
3. *Family pressures.* Extent to which external factors (illness, absence of father, financial problems, etc.) are present to intensify negative reactions in the home.
4. *Life partner.* Degree to which youth wonder or think about finding the "right one" to marry.
5. *Lack of self-confidence.* Degree to which one is anxious about making mistakes and being ridiculed by others.
6. *Academic problems.* Concern over school studies and one's ability. A fear of failing to do as well as one should.
7. *Personal faults.* Disappointment over not having lived up to one's ideals of personal living. Feelings of guilt.
8. *Classroom relationships.* A feeling of not being accepted by others while at school, that one is an outsider, lonely and unnecessary to a group.
9. *National issues.* Fear over what is happening nationwide coupled with a deep sensitivity to current injustices.
10. *God relationship.* A feeling of being out of touch with God and being troubled by it.

Beliefs and Values

11. *Interest in help.* Degree to which one might expect youth to participate in opportunities provided by the church.
12. *Maturity of values.* Perceived ability to delay immediate drives and resist outer pressures in favor of moving toward goals of one's own choosing.
13. *Orientation for change.* Degree to which youth's opinions on national issues tend to be more or less liberal in comparison to traditional attitudes.
14. *Moral responsibility.* Degree of importance youth give to being their brother's keeper and living under a sense of God's authority.
15. *Meaningful life.* Importance accorded a life of service, responsible living toward others, meaningful work, wisdom, honesty, a relationship with God, and giving and receiving love.
16. *Religious participation.* Degree of involvement in the life, faith, and activities of the institutional church.
17. *Social action.* Extent to which youth are helping through small deeds of kindness and participating in activities labeled social action.
18. *Self-regard.* Degree to which youth accept themselves as persons of worth and possibility.
19. *Human relations.* Attitudes of openness and kindness toward people of different nationalities, race, or religion.
20. *God awareness.* Extent to which youth are aware of God in their lives and believe that he is an ever-present reality.
21. *Biblical concepts.* Extent to which youth reject statements of a generalized religion and, in doing so, reflect their perception of a particularized, biblical faith.

Perception

22. *Youth group vitality.* Degree to which the youth are impressed by the climate of acceptance and sense of mission

that characterizes their church youth group.

23. *Adult caring.* Extent to which the youth are impressed by the attitudes of caring and concern that characterize the adult congregation.

24. *Family social concerns.* Youth's perception of the extent to which their parents and family are responsive to human need and involved in helping activities.

25. *Frankness.* Openness in admitting what is uncomplimentary.

These twenty-five recognizable characteristics organize themselves into five distinct and quite interpretable groups, or constellations. Through a computer process known as second-order factor analysis the magnetic attraction of one characteristic for its closest relatives produces these families of clusters.[3] Each combination of characteristics defines an area of great concern in the lives of young people:

Self-esteem
Family unity and well-being
Welfare of people
Personal advantage
Personal faith

How Authoritative Are the Data?

The detailed answer to this question can be found in another publication, *Manual for Youth Research Survey: Section 4* (Strommen and Gupta 1971).

The data closely approximate what is broadly or generally true in fact. Of course, optical scanners cannot always read the marks of youthful respondents; people who describe their feelings are not always accurate in what they say about themselves; the sample is not a precise random one drawn in proportion to the size of all denominational groups, and so on. But the empirical checks reported in the *Manual* show the data to be highly reliable and valid.

Underlying the discussion in this book are three assumptions:

1. that young people can be insightful and their reports valid; that they can report the conscious derivatives of unconscious motivations; that defense mechanisms, self-deception, rationalization do not dominate most young people enough to invalidate their total self-report;

2. that adolescent psychodynamics are evidenced by verbally expressed problems that tend to cluster symptomatically around an underlying concern (this means that from problem items can be inferred psychologically significant concerns);

3. that a knowledge of youth's concerns is important to an effective youth ministry (unless information is related to real interests and has immediate meaning it will be forgotten or perceived in distorted form).

Three cautions. First, this book is based on one kind of research data, namely, self-report. This means that our knowledge is limited to what church youth *said* they believe, value, opine, and do. Second, the data is cross-sectional in time and limited to correlational information; therefore the data cannot tell what *caused* what. Third, groups formed by the cries do overlap. Though most youth express predominantly one cry, some youth make several cries in somewhat equal proportions.

Who Are the Young People in the Study?

In this book you listen to a nationwide group of high-school age youth, randomly selected from among American Baptist, Roman Catholic (parochial school), United Methodist, Southern Baptist, and Young Life participants; samples were also taken from regional groups of Presbyterian, Lutheran, Church of Christ, Evangelical Covenant, and Episcopal youth to round out a fair sampling. Girls outnumber boys in a ratio of 54 percent to 46 percent, and sophomores slightly outnumber the other three high-school grades, but neither sex nor grade is markedly out of proportion (25 percent freshmen, 27 percent sophomores, 26 percent juniors, and 22 percent seniors).

Special efforts were made to include minority groups, residents of inner-city areas, and nonattending church youth. Though one is never 100 percent successful in recruiting participants, at least three out of four on membership rolls did cooperate—a better batting average than most surveys can report.

Were our participants honest in their self-reports? Or did they press for a halo effect, saying what they think religious people want to hear? Though pretense is always an issue, we found that a pledge of confidentiality ("only a computer will see your answers") plus a group-administered test situation did encourage a sense of anonymity. Our checks on frankness lead us to believe our participants spoke with candor.

Are Church Youth Different?

Some people assume that church youth are different from their peers. The director of one large foundation calls them the "good kids who have no problems." Some prominent businessmen refer to them as the rear guard of today's youth, a reflection of the past.

More myths are circulated about church youth than the facts support. In fact, to apply any one label to all church youth is impossible; our study shows them to be remarkably, refreshingly diverse.

If we are determined to compare church youth and the nonchurched, we can draw some information from the study itself. Within the sample are (1) 811 who rarely or never attend church and 6,239 who sometimes or often do, and (2) 732 whose parents belong to no church and 6,088 whose parents do.

Comparison of the groups tells us that church and nonchurch youth are alike in their reactions to common adolescent problems such as lack of parental understanding, dating problems, lack of self-confidence, academic problems, and classroom relationships.

It also reveals considerable similarity in political and/or social attitudes, although church youth are probably less conservative politically and less willing to preserve the status quo than other Americans. One can expect more church youth to favor progressive political action and to protest obvious dishonesties.

Church youth are probably more people oriented. In their attitudes toward the poor and minorities they resemble college students, ages nineteen to twenty-four, the most liberal group among youth.

If church youth are in any way a unique subculture, it is in their beliefs and values. Church youth and those outside the community of faith differ sharply in sense of moral responsibility; desire for a meaningful life; religious participation; social action; self-regard; feeling for people; God-awareness; and a positive orientation toward the congregation, youth group, and family.

Solid evidence tells us that church youth identify more with their parents; more of them say they have values, attitudes, and life qualities that are the same as those of their parents. The same has become true for high-school youth generally. A 1983 survey of American youth by the National Association of Secondary School Principals showed that a clear majority of students are willing to adopt the views of their parents on eight major issue areas, of which drug usage, education, religion, and careers are examples. In 1988, the same was true. Three out of four high school seniors agreed with their parents on such topics as careers, use of marijuana, use of drugs, values, education, and religion. Interestingly, this proportion of agreement marks an increase over a fourteen-year period. In 1973 the same survey found only one-half the youth agreeing with their parents (Bachman et al, 1988, 174–176). This is a significant development for American youth in general.

With contrasts in beliefs and values come contrasts in way of life. The lower incidence of premarital sex, drinking, and drug usage among youth of the church compared with that of the nonchurch group shows an ability or willingness to delay gratification that is related to what church youth value and believe; a personal faith in Jesus Christ makes a great difference in way of life and outlook on life.[4]

What Is the Useful Life of the 1970 Data?

Anyone who works with youth knows that times are changing, that "they didn't do it that way when I was young." This awareness poses the questions: Are today's youth radically different from youngsters of ten years ago, twenty years ago? Ten or fifteen years from now will there be similar differences?

The answer to these queries is yes if changing fads and moods are one's index, but no if one looks beneath the surface of change. Values, beliefs, attitudes, and concerns are remarkably consistent, irrespective of time, culture, or location. Low self-esteem troubles youth of Asia just as it does those in America; it crops up in diaries of youth from the fourth, sixteenth, and twentieth centuries. The twenty-five characteristics listed earlier are not unique to any one culture or period.

When an older version of the Youth Research Survey was translated into the Batak language for a study of students at Nommensen University (Indonesia) in 1966, only 7 of the 520 items then in use were considered inappropriate to that culture. Though the students were involved in the revolutionary activity of unseating Sukarno from his throne and radically changing the political situation, their reported concerns, values, beliefs, and feelings were similar to those of students in American church colleges.

There *are* changes today, obvious ones, but their importance has been overstressed in relation to the unchanging dynamics of behavior. Certain universal characteristics, patterns of behavior, and ways of looking at life continue to typify the adolescent and tell *why* he acts as he does. Knowledge of these dynamics can counterbalance our preoccupation with *how* youth are behaving.

There are those who hold that the unprecedented events of the sixties prove that we are seeing a new breed. Anthropologist

Margaret Mead contends that events between 1950 and 1970 have irrevocably altered relationships and ushered in a new age. She believes that between generations a break has occurred that is planetary, universal, and new to history. Everyone born and bred before World War II, she says, is an immigrant in time who cannot know what his children experientially know.

Using a national sample of church people, we tested Mead's theory and failed to find the radical break she claims.[5] Using fifty-two scales that measure differences at two-year intervals for a population varying in age between fifteen and sixty-five, we found no differences on two-fifths of the measures. Of the remaining three-fifths the extreme variation in degree and location of tension between age generations makes it evident that tension (let alone an open break) is pertinent only to certain characteristics. At best the "new breed" theory applies to a small subculture of high-school or college students; at worst it is another stereotype that does not fit the majority of American youth.

Our evidence leads to the conclusion that any relational gap between youth and parents is the same one that older adults knew as young people.

Are the cries of youth described in this book unique to this day? If intensity of outcry is the issue, then we might say yes. Today's youth seem to know more anxiety than those of former years and seem to have more freedom to speak their minds.

But if the substance is the issue, then I would say no. In my opinion the five cries described in this book are universal and timeless expressions of need or values—they are the ways in which all youth are alike. Our analyses of trends over a fifteen year period as well as findings from 1990 studies of church and public school youth show how this is true.

2. Cry of Self-Hatred

I yell inside my empty cave and my answer is an echo, an echo of cold words and cold pain.

Habel

This chapter describes the unvoiced cry that seriously haunts the lives of one young person in five. It rises out of feelings of worthlessness, self-criticism, and loneliness.

The cry of low self-esteem, plaintive and often irritating, is not always easy to understand. We notice a person acting as though he considers himself the most important person in the group. We sense a certain phoniness in his behavior but fail to recognize the feelings of inadequacy that prompt his look-at-me actions.

Fostering self-esteem is an important goal for home and church. Given a congenial atmosphere and reaffirming adults, youth can change their self-perceptions and gain a new outlook on life. The awareness that one is loved by God and other people can be encouraged.

John seems a quiet, shy young man, all eyeglasses and floppy blond hair, sitting in the tenor section of the church choir. He excites neither trouble nor the interest of the people around him. His infrequent talk is usually about sports events. It is extremely important to him that his team should win; a loss by his school's team, his state university team, or his favorite professional team can make him morose and depressed for days. Not precisely unfriendly, he seldom opens a conversation, and when he responds to someone else's remarks he talks a bit too loudly, a bit too fast, as though people might not hear him out unless he gets it all said in a rush of words.

John is a victim of strong feelings of worthlessness. Guilt, anxiety, and loneliness plague him constantly. He is given to erotic fantasies and frequent daydreams as a way of living out his desires of being a hero. Guilt over masturbation results in a tendency to downgrade himself severely. He is usually a loner, unwilling to force his company on others, sure that he is unworthy of their attention. But when he is with others he tries hard to please or amuse them; their favorable attention, or their laughter, is of great value to him. Seeing himself as a loser, he identifies with athletic teams and depends on them for a vicarious sense of victory and his own temporary importance.

Wherever he goes John constantly and silently cries out, "I'm worthless!" The great, urgent need of his life is to be someone he himself could love and respect.

Self-esteem, "feeling good about oneself," is a vital element in a person's life. When it is lacking, alienating and self-destructive types of behavior appear. When it is present, life takes on excitement and purpose.

People with a sense of worth do more than accept their strengths and weaknesses. They also reflect patient hope and quiet conviction that they will grow and improve. Though they may criticize themselves they do so without condemnation; though they may admit limitations they do so without feeling inadequate. Because they feel good about themselves they are free to become involved in meeting the needs of others.

There are few sufferings equal to the pain of feeling no good, unattractive, inadequate, worthless. Kind words spoken to John, for instance, are immediately discounted. "You're just trying to make me feel good." He is prevented from reaching out to others for companionship; he is sure nobody wants him around. "Who'd want me to come to the party? Who'd want me to join the team? Who'd want me to call them up?" Constantly and consistently John and others like him cut themselves off from the healing qualities of the everyday human associations that those who have a sense of worth enjoy and take for granted.

Feelings of worthlessness often make people turn on themselves in anger. Then the cry becomes a mixture of worthlessness, self-hatred, and loneliness. As the most commonly voiced and the most intensely felt of the five cries, it is the first to be discussed.

Three Self-Relational Characteristics

Feelings begin in the brain, in a person's perceptions. A woman worried sick over the possibility of a malignancy is suddenly relieved and exuberant when the doctor tells her the lump is benign. A change in perception brings a change in feelings.

Perceptions held over a period of time tend to harden into a fairly persistent combination of reactions or tendencies. To know a person's tendencies is to understand how he or she will respond to others and to life itself. We say, "You better be careful how you talk to her. She has a tendency to be easily hurt." Or, "He has a tendency to think nobody likes him."

Of the many tendencies, or dispositions, that characterize human beings, the most powerful are the self-relational, which have to do with feelings about oneself. More than any other feeling, these touch the innards of a person's emotional life and spark the glands and the smooth muscles of the autonomic nervous system. When feelings of self-criticism, lack of self-confidence, and low self-worth pummel a person long and hard, they leave their mark on physical well-being and effective functioning. Often this involves skin disorders, physical ailments, or debilitating psychological states; linked also are drug use, suicide, and self-defeating behavior.

What did we find in our study that helps to understand this first cry? We found eight feelings and concerns clustered together to form a constellation of characteristics. Three are feelings about oneself (self-relational), and five are concerns about others (other-relational). They intertwine with sufficient intensity to qualify as a distinct area of need.

The interrelationship of the three self-relational characteristics is shown in the upper part of figure 1. Distress over personal

Figure 1. Characteristics of that Worthless Feeling

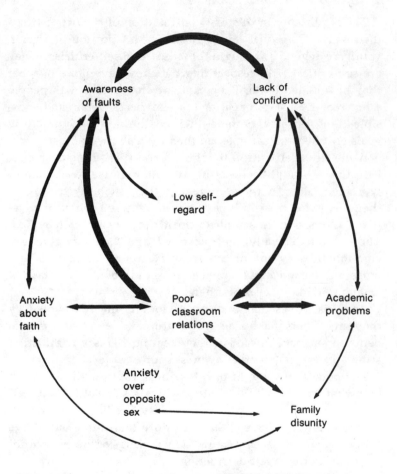

Heaviness of arrow indicates strength of intercorrelation.

faults (self-criticism) and lack of self-confidence (personal anxiety) undermine feelings of self-regard; as self-criticism and anxiety mount, self-regard drops lower and lower.

Distress over Personal Faults

The big brother in this first constellation of characteristics is distress over personal faults. A significant portion of church youth are dogged by thoughts of failure and self-criticism. They are self-critical with respect to what they have done or what they have failed to do. They compare themselves with people who excel in an area appealing to them; perfection in an impossible number of areas becomes their goal. Aiming for unrealistic goals only serves to exaggerate their own shortcomings.

A cluster of self-critical thoughts forms this strong characteristic. In these youth feelings of guilt and remorse are abundantly evident along with awareness of their inability to forgive themselves. Yet the youth most troubled by self-criticism are as likely as others in the sample to affirm they are forgiven by God. Though intellectually they acknowledge God's forgiveness, emotionally they do not live in an awareness of God's acceptance but remain preoccupied with standards and the task of "making it" in the eyes of others.

Analysis shows that one out of four is much troubled by thoughts of personal blame. An additional one in two admits to being somewhat bothered by these feelings. This is an affliction known in varying degrees by most youth.

The persistent thought of self-critical youth is this: "I don't like what I do. I can't live up to my ideals." The attendant feelings are insecurity, self-pity, and jealousy. Predictably such feelings generate thoughts of suicide. More than three out of five (62 percent) of those *most* troubled by feelings of low esteem admit to thoughts of self-destruction.[1]

A qualifier seems necessary at this point because self-criticism is admittedly necessary for progress and growth. A self-critical individual is the one most likely to see moral obligations and carry them out. That person is most likely to rise to positions of leadership because he or she can see what is lacking and what needs to be improved in both himself or herself and others. The issue is the *degree* of self-criticism operating in the individual.

Most adolescents go through periods of feeling quite worthless, especially following some disappointing experience in their friendships or after having failed to measure up to others in school grades or sports activities. Such feelings usually pass over like clouds. If they persist and dominate, they become destructive, because excessive self-criticism tears down self-esteem and interferes with relationships. Such youth especially need to experience the acceptance and love of others. An atmosphere of mutual acceptance can free them to deal with their negative perceptions and feelings of personal guilt.

Lack of Self-Confidence

Jean quit her Bible discussion group, and no one knew why. Though very shy she had seemed interested. Later she admitted, "I quit because class makes me angry—angry with myself. I wanted to take part in the discussion, but I didn't dare." Jean added that she was afraid that anything she said would sound trite or ridiculous, that she was not comfortable just sitting there. "I was afraid someone would call on me and smoke me out. It angers me that I cannot think of anything to say like the rest."

Lack of self-confidence is a top-ranking characteristic in feelings of worthlessness. It is living with the nagging fear, "I'm going to blow it. I'll pull a boner, and everyone will laugh at me." Unchecked, the fear goes a step further and actually inhibits the flow of ideas. If called on to express an opinion, Jean knows her mind will dart frantically around and find nothing to say. This frightening prospect is enough to stop the timid from coming to discussion meetings.

Three out of four of our respondents (74 percent) are bothered in some degree by feelings of personal anxiety. Only one in four is relatively free of them. The greatest threats are posed by class recitations or activities where one can be humiliated or seen as a failure. Because these youth are thin-skinned and upset by adverse criticism, they fear making mistakes or being seen as "getting out of line." It is hard to overstate their embarrassment over a gurgling stomach, a mispronounced word, or a note that is warbled off-key.

They are convinced they lack talent and realize their dependence on the praise of others. Even as they "bow and scrape" they are bothered by the knowledge of it.

Youth lacking self-confidence screen out activities where they might fail. They won't try out for the school play, work on an important committee, or join in a spontaneous game of volleyball or softball. At a party they'll decline the new game or dance. "Oh, no," they will protest, "I'm no good at that kind of stuff. I couldn't do that." Discounting their ability without even a trial, such young people cut themselves off not only from the fun of an activity but also from the possibility for personal growth.

The correlation between lack of self-confidence and personal faults (i.e., the degree to which they covary) is high ($r = .73$). In all probability the two feelings interact reciprocally to increase each other. Those who are harsh in their self-criticism usually assume that others are judging them in the same way. Therefore they tend to be uneasy in group situations and carefully guarded lest they be viewed negatively. This self-consciousness in turn becomes the basis for another round of self-criticism. Such people regretfully note how easily others are able to speak and are angered by their own cloddishness and lack of verbal grace. A college freshman expressed the fear of ridicule and humiliation that underlies a lack of confidence:

> I wish
> That I could
> say what
> I wish
> so that you
> will not laugh
> at me.
>
> > And you say you would
> > not laugh
> > out loud

but inside you would
be laughing
so loud
that I could hear
it from there, too.
So I will remain
quiet
exposing my wishes only
to this paper
which cannot laugh.

Sabine

In 1965 Dr. Morris Rosenberg reported a prize-winning study of 5,042 adolescents in the state of New York, showing the close relationship between low self-confidence and anxiety. According to Rosenberg, an adolescent suffering from pangs of self-contempt may (1) retreat into the world of imagination where he or she can dream of himself or herself as worthy, or (2) put up a false front to convince others that he or she is worthy. Both responses tend to separate the person from others.

Other dynamics may also be involved. An adolescent boy caught in these feelings may concentrate on being very good in order to be loved, on being strong in order to be admired, or on being capable in order to be praised. Standards, rules, and regulations may become too important as measures of worth or achievement. A girl believes that she is liked not for what she *is* but for the good things she *does;* thus the more she achieves, the more others will like her. Instead of moving toward greater self-expression and self-realization, she sees self-effacement as goodness and withdrawal from threat as freedom.

Low Self-Regard

The third characteristic is perceiving oneself as a person of low worth, a person without importance.

About one-half of our respondents admit to this perception. Of these, 15 percent say their perception has become a continuous pattern of reactions. They tend to feel lonely, uncomfortable about the future, and bored with life; they speak about competence, talent, and ability as qualities that others, not they, possess.

An inevitable result of low self-regard is loneliness. A young person with a negative view of himself does not enjoy being alone; he succumbs to thoughts such as these: "I'm not fit to be with. But I have to be with myself. There's no way I can get away. Maybe if I am with other people, it will help take my mind off me. But how can I be with people? They don't want me. I'm not fit to be with."

Few of the lonely see life as a celebration. Most seek anonymity through adopting a public pose and keeping people at arm's length. The jovial heavyweight who joshes about her obesity confesses in private that her joking is a cover-up. She is really a lonely person. Loneliess influences personal estimates of life (see table 1).

Table 1
Influence of Loneliness

	Percentage Answering Yes		
Item	Lonely N = 1,305	Sometimes Lonely N = 2,844	Not Lonely N = 2,854
I find life exciting and full of fun	30	49	68
I feel that my future is in good hands	32	48	68
I feel no one knows me	64	37	27

The big issue for most lonely youth is having friends. Most (87 percent) say that outside their families they really belong to no one group and are bothered to some degree by the lack of friends at school (versus 55 percent of the nonlonely).

It is interesting that most lonely youth report having *some* close friends. Sixteen percent report as many as ten close friends "who really care" about them. Apparently loneliness is not cured by company, nor does solitude necessarily increase it. Aloneness is more than physical separation in life; it is akin to the fear of nonbeing or meaninglessness so often identified with the alienation of the twentieth century, which Kierkegaard believed was cured only through an identification with God.

The issue is not so much friends as the ability to commit oneself to another. To know the trust of deep attachments a young person must entrust himself to others. Inability to do so robs him of the affection he needs so desperately. Unable to open his life to others in a caring and loving way, he does not experience the love and affection of others, which could give him a sense of well-being and worth. Nancy expressed it well:

> Standing apart
> I heard you say hello
> it was sweet of you to try
> but I was (after all)
> standing apart.
> Nancy Nelson, age seventeen

Five Other-Relational Characteristics

Low self-esteem inhibits relationships, and poor human relationships erode self-esteem. Attitudes toward the opposite sex, academic problems, parents, and God affect and are affected by self-perception. Figure 1 shows how these additional five characteristics interrelate with the first three.

Classroom Relationships

Most church youth find school relationships bothersome to some degree. They feel critical of insensitive classmates and unsympathetic teachers. They are bothered by the "pressure to do what others do" and are disappointed by the way they succumb—"I often act different from what I really am"—(see table 2).

Table 2
Concern over Classroom Relationships among Church Youth
Ecumenical Sample
(N = 7,050)

Classroom Relationships	
Item	Percentage Concerned*
Classmates at school could be more friendly	53
In a group I often act different from what I really am	52
Some classmates are inconsiderate of my feelings	51
There are cliques (closed groups) in my school	51
I feel pressure at school to do what others do	50
There are not enough opportunities to be with a mixed group (boys and girls) in social activities	41
Some teachers are sarcastic and critical of what I do	38
Some of my teachers do not understand me	37
My interests are often different from those of others my age	35

*Very much, quite a bit, somewhat

Academic Problems

Many educators oppose the use of grades in evaluating academic performance because of their impact on the self-esteem and motivation of young people. To what extent do low grades increase youth's feelings of low self-esteem? Our data shows that students who get low grades, who are unable to concentrate on their school work, and who worry about their academic performance usually rank low in self-esteem. Lack of competence, skill, or application in academic matters is linked with a low self-image. One can speculate in several directions:

1. teachers' evaluations (grades) lower or raise a student's self-esteem; or
2. feelings of low esteem lead to the fantasizing and daydreaming that prevent concentration—with resulting lower grades; or

3. less academically able youth are more troubled with low self-esteem whether they are in school or not.

Though our data shows that low grades bother recipients more than most adults suppose, low grades are not a major cause of low self-esteem. If grades were not given at school, it is likely that a youth troubled by low estimate of self would continue to feel worthless. Other comparisons would still lead him or her to say,"I am not as smart as others my age."

Abrasive parent-youth relationships also influence grades. Youth with low grades report more conflicts at home and express more concern over their parents' relationship with each other.

Our data show differences in the way of life of academic low-achievers that bear a strong relation to grades (see table 3). Differences in values and socioeconomic level are also associated with grade differences. Thirty-eight percent of youth with excellent grades had fathers in a profession and college-educated mothers, as compared to 14 percent of youth with low grades. It is evident that factors other than native ability are linked to academic achievement, and factors other than grades to low self-esteem.

Table 3
Percentage Saying Yes to Questionable Activities

| Item | Grades in School | | | | |
	Very Low N=157	Below Avg. N=456	Avg. N=2,564	Above Avg. N=2,904	Excell. N=761
I have taken things that did not belong to me	75	68	57	48	41
I sometimes get "high" on alcoholic beverages	61	45	35	26	22
Sexual intercourse on a date (is an option)	33	18	16	11	11
Use of drugs (is an issue)	36	20	12	9	7

Anxiety about God Relationship

Low self-regard is related to anxiety about one's faith and a troubled awareness of distance and alienation from God. Whether experienced as spiritual lonesomeness, inability to live up to one's religious convictions, or a concern over life after death, anxiety over the God relationship characterizes low self-esteem youth.

In a 1963 study, *Profiles of Church Youth,* I found a correlation ($r = .49$) between the dimensions feelings of inadequacy and God relationship. Ten years later, using different youth populations, the same dimensions emerged with a similar correlation ($r = .40$). Apparently youth with low self-esteem are anxious about all of life's realities. How a sense of alienation includes the God relationship is indicated by the percentage of friendless youth who cannot believe in a personal caring God (see table 4).

Table 4
Percentage Saying Yes to Faith Items

	Number of Friends	
	None	10 or More
Item	N=359	N=1,769
Jesus is the divine Son of God	44	72
God cares for me in a special way	45	75
I have a sense that my prayers have been answered by God	40	70

In another study Peter Benson and Bernard Spilka found a fairly high association ($r = .46$) between self-esteem and viewing God as a loving and accepting person. Youth of low self-esteem tend to see God as vindictive and controlling. Apparently their inner needs call for a more rejecting God who punishes rather than loves the evildoer.[2]

Concern over Family Relationships

Rosenberg, in his study of self-esteem, gave special attention to the effect of parental disinterest. He focused upon parents' knowledge of children's friends, parents' interest in their child's report cards, and the degree to which the young person participates in dinner conversations. He concluded with this statement:

Whether one belongs to the upper, upper-middle, lower-middle, or lower social classes; whether one is a Protestant, Catholic, or Jew; whether one is male or female; whether one lives in a large city, a medium sized community, or small town—whichever of these conditions obtain, the result is essentially the same: if the parent manifests indifference to the child, that child is less likely to have a high level of self-regard.

He also found that low self-esteem was likelier if a mother were indifferent to low grades than if she nagged about them. In other words, the most telling comment of low self-esteem youth with respect to parents was, "She seldom commented on my work."

Overstrictness is also associated with low self-perception. Kirkpatrick has a theory that parents who feel inferior are sensitive to their modest achievements and limited importance in the scheme of things. When children fail to obey or show proper respect for their authority, it is seen as another sign of their own failure and calls up strong emotions. Cockiness in the child begets a strict, punitive reaction in the parent who sees it not as a compensation for inferiority feelings but as a threat to his or her authority (Sebald 1968). Such parents may also be preoccupied with standards; because they cannot accept themselves they have unrealistic expectations for themselves and their children.

Since overstrictness is reported by two out of five church young people, one can speculate that large numbers of parents are insecure, rule-oriented people. Overcontrolling and overprotective, they serve as models for their children, while tending to pass on their own low self-esteem. A local congregational ministry must take seriously the low self-esteem of parents.

Relationship with Opposite Sex

Most youth worry about relating successfully to members of the opposite sex and eventually finding the right person for a happy marriage. To have dates is for many a measure of worth. Fifty-one percent of church youth spent time every day (or quite often) thinking about "how to keep boys/girls interested in me." Almost half (47 percent) spent time every day (or quite often) wondering "whether or not I will find a life partner." Concern over finding a life partner correlates with two major indicants of low self-esteem, namely, personal faults ($r = .49$) and lack of self-confidence ($r = .40$). These correlations are highly significant in light of the importance dating holds for many youth.

We have described youth's feelings of worthlessness and have shown how they affect all relationships, creating a kind of cosmic alienation.

The hopeful thesis of this analysis is that friends, teachers, parents, and God can establish a quality of relationship that enhances feelings of esteem, changes the way of perceiving the self, and helps young people to believe in their worth and significance.

This is what the gospel seeks to do—to convince a person that he or she is loved by God and is an important member of God's family. When such a message dawns on a person who feels worthless, it is "good news" indeed. The change in perception leads to a new outlook on life, emergence from the cave of loneliness, and a coming back into touch with self, others, and God.

How many youth are we talking about who have a special need for such a ministry?

Proportion of Youth Having Low Self-Esteem

One out of five (20 percent) of all youth in our survey are buoyed by a sense of positive self-esteem. If we drop one criterion (e.g., high grades), we find that two in five (37 percent) are relatively free of self-critical attitudes and thoughts of suicide and hold themselves in relatively high self-regard. On the other hand, tragically, 20 percent of church youth harbor thoughts of severe self-criticism and even suicide. In 1988 the same proportion of high school seniors were struggling with thoughts of worthlessness, loneliness and dissatisfaction (Bachman et al, 1988, 195–197).

On the average, one out of five church youth enjoys high self-esteem, and one out of five suffers under the heavy hand of self-accusation. For the majority of church youth it is a concern of varying proportions.[3]

It is well to observe that low self-esteem is passed on in families. Anxiety and stress characterize all ages; defensive behavior is not uniquely adolescent. Youth differ primarily in that their emotions are more volatile and their behavior more extreme and less controlled. Practically speaking, a ministry that is effective for youth applies also to their parents.

Has the Cry Changed?

When Daniel Offer and his research team compared normal adolescents of the sixties and the seventies, they found that teenagers of the late seventies felt more vulnerable than their peers of a generation earlier.[4] Their studies showed that normal adolescents of the sixties had a more positive social image than those of a decade later (Offer, Astrov, and Howard 1981).

When we dipped into our data bank in 1977 we found that the cry had not changed. For these first seven years, on five dimensions of self-hatred, scores of the 6,833 youth who took the survey in 1977 were identical with those of 1970. The five dimensions or measures were as follows:

personal faults
lack of self-confidence
classroom relationships
God relationships
family unity

Self-regard, a sixth dimension, did increase 2.1 standard points to show that more youth in 1977 than 1970 felt good about themselves. Though the increase was statistically significant, we deemed it too small to alter our conclusion of "no change" based on the first five measures.

In 1980 3,340 Lutheran students (a complete census of parochial school youth) took the Youth Research Survey, giving us a chance to assess possible changes in the cry of self-hatred since 1970 for Lutheran youth.[5] Interestingly measures of these three dimensions remained identical:

family unity
lack of self-confidence
classroom relationships

And scores on three others show a slight improvement:

personal faults
God relationship
self-regard

Because scales measuring these dimensions are highly reliable, a slight improvement must be acknowledged because the shift could not have occurred by chance. In spite of this slight shift in half the measures, one can still say the cry in 1980 has remained relatively unchanged since 1970.

What about youth in public schools? Have their feelings about themselves changed over a 13-year period? Knowing how youth suicides have increased, one expects some change in the number troubled by the dynamic of self-hatred. The answer is "not much."

A 13-year comparison (1976–1988) of seniors randomly selected from United States public schools showed no marked change. The only change was a slight improvement in seniors' attitudes of loneliness. Fewer felt lonely or wish they had more friends. These shifts in seniors' feelings about themselves during the 13-year period were statistically significant for only one of the five items (table 5). From a practical standpoint, one must conclude that the cry is unchanged. It remains a troublesome concern for approximately the same proportion of youth in 1988 as in 1976.

The slight increase in self-esteem noted in the studies quoted above become more apparent in Gupta's trend analysis of change over a fifteen-year period for church youth. His comparison of 2,200 church youth responding in 1988 with the original sample of 7,050 youth in 1970 shows an advance in self-esteem on all six measures:

self-regard
lack of self-confidence
personal faults
God relationship
classroom relationships
family unity

Significantly the advance is greatest on self-regard, with a lessening of concern over one's personal faults and God relationship. The improvement in scores of this trend analysis could not have happened by chance once in a hundred times.[7]

Table 5
Thirteen-Year Comparison of Seniors' Attitudes toward Self

Item	Percentage Agreeing		
	1977 N =3,000	1988 N =3,350	Percent Difference
I take a positive attitude toward myself	82%	81%	−1
A lot of times I feel lonely	38	35	−3*
I often feel left out of things	32	33	+1
I often wish I had more friends	51	50	−1
Sometimes I think I am no good	26	25	−1

*statistically significant at 1 percent level

Changes among Church Youth

Fewer American youth and church youth are bothered by the dynamic of self-hatred. This advance at a time one would expect a reverse development among American youth may be a result of the many program efforts to raise youth's self-esteem. Such programs have been introduced in the public schools as an important preventive measure to forestall drug and alcohol abuse.

The striking advance in self-regard among church youth coupled with their lessened concern over personal faults and their relationship to God may indicate youth's greater attention to a gospel of forgiveness and grace. The gain is a significant one that may well reflect a greater gospel orientation among the 1985 youth. It could, however, be caused by a combination of other factors.

From a practical standpoint has the cry changed? Hardly. Although fewer are bothered by this dynamic, the same approximate number are troubled over the various dimensions of self-hatred. Though an improvement is discernible in self-esteem, the fact remains that approximately one in five church youth are troubled by low self-regard and feelings of loneliness. They are a significant group. To their numbers must be added the school dropouts who never make the senior year and those youth from troubled families who drop out of the fellowship of a congregation. A disproportionate number of these youth struggle with the cry of self-hatred.

Youth's Awareness of Their Need

Do low self-esteem youth want to change the way they relate to themselves, to others, and to God? We offered survey statements that describe opportunities a church might provide (e.g., to learn to make friends and be a friend). Response possibilities were as follows:

1. No—I am not interested in the opportunity.
2. Much—I am very much interested and would go out of my way to participate.
3. Some—I am interested but would not make a special effort to participate.

Which of the forty opportunities proved most attractive to the low self-esteem youth drawn from the ecumenical sample? (These are the 572 youth who score high on personal faults and lack of self-confidence and low on self-regard.)

Their highest preference is a tie (78 percent): to find meaning in life and to learn how to make friends and be a friend. Second out of forty possibilities are opportunities that involve leaving their public posture and taking off their masks. Three out of four want to be "more of the real me" in a group. They want help in finding friends and learning to be friends to members of both sexes. Friends are to them what bread is to the hungry and clothes to the naked. What is needed is a ministry of friendship—activities that bring people together to interact.

Three out of four want to be part of a caring, accepting group. Two out of three want a group that, in addition to offering acceptance, also allows members to confront one another with an honest, frank sharing of personal feelings. They want small-group experiences that get at the feeling level and help them to come out from under their public posture.

One opportunity especially singled out by the low-esteem youth (N=572) was this one: "I would like to find a way to deal with my lack of self-confidence." Next was a related item, "I would like assistance in understanding myself and the reason for my problems." Sixty-one percent declared much interest in "experiencing a closer relationship with God." Table 6 gives dramatic evidence of the kinds of help these youth would like.

Table 6
Opportunities Preferred by Low Self-Esteem Youth
N=572

Item	Percentage Much Interested
Relationship with Others	
To learn how to make friends and be a friend	78
To learn to be more of the real me when I am with other people	77
To learn to get along better with members of the opposite sex	75
To experience acceptance in a group of people who really care about each other	74
Group meetings where people feel free to say what they really think and are honest about what bothers them	66
To learn how to be a friend to those who are lonely and rejected	60
Recreation and social activities where youth get acquainted	58

Relationship with God

To find meaning and purpose in my life	78
To experience a closer relationship with God	61
To find a good basis for deciding what is right and wrong	60

Relationship with Self

Assistance in understanding myself and the reasons for my problems	72
To find a way to deal with my lack of self-confidence	69
To learn to live with the pressures people place on me (friends, school, parents, church, etc.)	64

Another indication of the help youth desire comes from the study Clergy-Youth Counseling Project funded by the National Institute of Mental Health. Four hundred high-school juniors in experimental congregations listed changes they wanted for themselves during the fifteen months of the project. Each listed two to five hoped-for changes (table 7).

A striking feature of this list is the high interest in bettering one's relationship with others, with God, and with oneself. The youth who described these three dimensions are typical and

Table 7
Hoped-for Changes of Four Hundred Youth

Hoped-for Changes	No. Times Mentioned by 400 Youth
Better relationships	681
Be a better Christian	318
Have better self-concept	276
Have more self-confidence	256
Do better in school	220
Be a better person	206
Overcome personal faults	192
Improved parent/family relationships	123
More involved in church	75
Better physical appearance	73
Improved personality	67

were not ones singled out because of low self-esteem. It seems that self-esteem and enhanced relationships are goals welcomed by most church youth.

In what direction does a parent or youth leader go to meet the needs that are overwhelmingly apparent?

An Appropriate Approach

The hope of the Christian church is that all people might love God, their neighbor, and themselves. Christ showed how these relationships intertwine when he said we are to love our neighbor as ourselves. The Apostle John added, "We love because he first loved us." Love begets love.

Through his incarnation and life Christ showed that God's message is communicated by showing it, living it, speaking it. It is a living Word that is to be heard, seen, felt, and experienced through another person. The essence of the message is what a little girl left in a note to her dad: "I love you—is that okay?"

The message, which people are to incarnate, centers in promise and possibilities—no person is a hopeless case. Possibilities for change are open to everyone because implicit in each of God's promises are the words "I am with you." The unique potential in a Christian ministry is the awareness of God working in man, inspiring both the will and the deed.

A Christian youth ministry should be an extension of one's theology. The accent should be not on problem solving (overcoming fears, gaining confidence, improving one's self-concept) but on helping youth to become aware of possibilities found in a relationship with Jesus Christ. This means communicating to youth that they are loved, are important, have potential, and can look forward to growth and positive change. A change in their awareness will come not through indoctrination or the repetition of words but through the "living words" of people who embody God's message. These hope-inspiring people, in imitation of Christ, are convinced there is hope for every person and that God's yes applies to everyone.

An incarnational theology and a sensitivity to low self-esteem youth lead to these warnings:

1. Obligations, expectations, and rules should be deemphasized in the way adults work with youth and in the content of their discussions. Low self-esteem people are constantly saying no about themselves. They do not need a louder negative voice.
2. A rules-oriented religion—which low self-esteem youth tend to accept—must be exposed as practical atheism by contrasting it with a gospel of affirmation.
3. The techniques of hearty encouragement, bushels of compliments, and a series of social gatherings are not enough. Low self-esteem youth need a community or small group where they can live in the awareness of being accepted.
4. Competitive activities (e.g., "head-trip" discussions or competitive sports) tend to encourage unfavorable comparisons and threaten the more anxious youth. Socializing activities should stress cooperative activities where no one loses and discussions where no one is seen as wrong.

Concern and Warmth, the Key Factors

A ministry (whether in home or church) that works toward greater self-esteem among youth and adults must create the conditions that are freeing and disarming to low self-esteem people. It must accent warmth and congeniality to counteract the chilling effects of an anxious and self-condemning spirit.

What is needed most are people who have found an identity in life and are willing to share themselves with others. The primary qualifications for such adults center in what they incarnate and believe, in being sensitive to others and open to their possibilities. They must be people who can step into another person's shoes and just as easily step back into their own.

The important factor in helping another person to esteem and a sense of identity is not problem-solving techniques or expertise. It is the empathic and warm relationship of a concerned person. In a sense the words said or the specific relating techniques used matter little so long as the interaction establishes a warm relationship. If the essentials in helping youth to a sense of personal significance are the human qualities of empathy, warmth, and genuineness, then untrained people, both youth and adults, can be helpful.

Elements Working for Self-Esteem

A climate of warmth encourages self-esteem in several ways. First, it frees the person to verbalize his feelings and to put into words the emotions churning inside. Once feelings can be articulated, dealt with rationally; the person can be guided by good sense and sound judgment instead of irrational drives. Second, a congenial affirming climate encourages one to accept new information about himself or herself, to hear God's promise, and to accept and acknowledge strengths and weaknesses. Hearing and experiencing love and acceptance changes a person's self-perception.

It is hard to overstate the importance of times when youth and adults can acknowledge their humanity through sharing honest doubts and irrational fears. There is a quiet release and growth as masks are removed and one finds acceptance and love. What must be fought in home and church is the attitude "You shouldn't talk like that," which drives emotions underground to continue their eroding effect on the human spirit. We cannot solve youth's problems or manipulate their growth; we can only provide conditions for growth—the warmth of caring spirits, inquiring minds, and awareness of God's message.

Effects of Mutual Interchange

Does mutuality really make a discernible difference in the lives of youth? Some evidence is available from the Clergy-Youth Counseling Project referred to earlier.

Youth of forty congregations in the Minneapolis–St. Paul area participated in a two-year study designed to test the effect of nonprofessionals interacting with youth. Young people in twenty congregations served as controls, and a second group from twenty randomly assigned congregations served as experimentals. All took the Youth Research Survey at the beginning, middle, and end of the project. The difference was that the experimentals had the choice of conversing with their pastors about their counseling profiles; congregational youth leaders had the stimulus of a group report on their youth and the encouragement to try out new ways to meet some of their expressed needs; parents in some of the experimental congregations enrolled in Parent Effectiveness Training and learned how to relate better to their youth.[8] These opportunities were optional and integrated into the normal program of the twenty experimental congregations. No one was asked to counsel a fixed number of times or to participate in any of the congregational activities.

Distress over personal faults and lack of self-confidence, academic problems, and classroom relationships dropped significantly among the experimental youth. Their gain in these aspects of self-esteem stood in contrast with youth in the control congregations. Clearly, increased adult interest and attention make a measurable impact on the lives of youth.

3. Cry of Psychological Orphans

My dad and I don't get along too
good the past couple of years. That's
why I'm out goofin' around tonight.
I think I'm afraid of my parents,
kinda, inside.

A seventeen-year-old boy

The most poignant cry is the sob of despair or shriek of sheer frustration among youth living in atmospheres of parental hatred and distrust. Often such distress ends in running away from home, delinquent behavior, suicide, or other self-destructive behavior. This chapter identifies the four major characteristics of such homes: family pressures; distress over relationships with parents; disappointment in family unity; and a negative perception of one's family social concerns. Because youth despairing over their family situation often think of suicide, we will also give consideration to this third highest killer of youth. The chapter ends with a section that briefly reviews elements that make for family health.

Characteristics of Family Conflict

In Robert Frost's poem "Death of the Hired Man" two characters each try to define the word *home*. Warren defines it as a kind of mechanical necessity, without any warmth or kindess:

Home is the place where, when you have to go there,
They have to take you in.

Mary, on the other hand, sees home as something akin to an earthly expression of God's grace:

I should have called it
Something you somehow haven't to deserve.

On every street there are homes of both kinds and others with all the gradations between. Young people go in and out of these homes every day and experience the powerful effect of their family's atmosphere.

This second of the five cries of youth rises from young people who desperately need the stability, support, and love of a home they "somehow haven't to deserve." The cry of these young people is, "I need to be part of a family where we love and accept and care about each other."

The young people of this chapter can be predictably placed in only one category—a troubled home situation. To any question relating to family they tend to give a negative response.

They answer as *youth whose preoccupation is their distressing family situation*. No other characteristics join this constellation—not even those related to self-esteem or religious faith; neither self-deprecation nor religious disinterest is uniquely found among these youth. Except for home life they are typical church youth. There is nothing in what they believe, value, think, or do that points a blaming finger at them for disruption in the home. It is probably the parents who are primarily responsible.

The need for help is so intense for some that, lacking the encouragement of adult friends and support groups, they may turn to irrational and tragic actions. One example is suicide; another is rebellious or delinquent behavior; yet another is running away to join some group whose way of life is part of the counterculture.

The distress of problems centering in the family is illustrated by skin-resistance data. Disturbed adolescents whose problems tend to center at home in active family conflict show greater skin reactivity than adolescents whose difficulties center outside the home. The feelings generated by tension between parents and siblings is so intense that the body registers the impact (Goldstein et al. 1970).

This chapter draws attention to psychological orphans who lack the support and love needed for healthy development and

Figure 2. Characteristics of Youth in Family Conflict

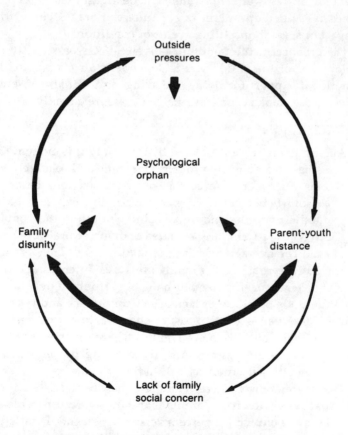

Heaviness of arrow indicates strength of intercorrelation.

identifies what may be needed in a ministry to these youth. Survey information will describe what racks the emotions of about one church youth in five.

Family Pressures

About 21 percent of our respondents have known separation or divorce of parents, illness, financial duress, parent-youth strife, absenteeism of the father, and serious difficulties due to such calamities as unemployment and death. In some cases pressures have piled up and the family suffers under the cumulative impact of several unsettling events or conditions.

Disturbance in the family negatively affects personality development of the child, who is dependent on his parents for emotional support for living, behaving, and thinking. We can take a closer look at some events that pressure a family.

Divorce/separation

Among the 8 percent isolated by this study it is evident that divorce has created many problems for some and relatively few problems for others. We can make generalizations based on comparisons between the 8 percent who have experienced divorce in their families and the remaining youth in the sample.

Youth whose parents are separated or divorced are more bothered than the average over lack of family unity. They are also more likely to report other family pressures. Interestingly they do not differ from all other youth in being troubled over lack of parental understanding or lack of self-confidence and personal faults. However, a third measure shows a lower estimate of worth among youth living in families where divorce or separation has become necessary. Also these young people do have more difficulty with their school studies.

The staying power of a religious faith may be indicated by the fact that fewer divorced parents than nondivorced parents are members of a church (55 percent versus 82 percent). Paralleling the less frequent church membership of divorced parents is a lower religious interest among their children when compared with all other church youth. Their lessened religious interest shows up in a variety of ways. Fewer youth of divorced parents than of nondivorced parents are interested in help from their church or participate actively in the life of the congregation. Fewer are charitable toward people commonly condemned or feel a sense of moral responsibility. Fewer are conscious of a personal, caring God, or report that their families go out of their way to help others.

A large and comprehensive study by Guidibaldi in 1983 compares fifth-grade children of divorced parents with peers of intact families. Boys of divorced parents contrast strikingly with fifth-grade boys of intact families on a variety of measures. They show less peer popularity, greater pessimism, lower scores in reading, math, and classroom conduct, and the greater likelihood of repeating a school grade. A consistent finding is that a boy in a single-mother family is more likely to be involved in aggressive acts toward his mother. Boys typically react to a single-mother family situation with aggression, whereas girls tend to react by being more helpful (Guidibaldi 1983).

In this study of church youth divorce emerges as one of many factors that disturb the families of youth. Because divorce is clearly understood, it will be used as a basis for comparison with other factors more disturbing to youth.

Family difficulties

Unfortunate as divorce may be, more discernible tension is associated with difficulties posed by prolonged illness, unemployment, death or injuries, or personal problems. Youth living under such pressures are more troubled with respect to all family relationships. As would be expected, self-regard goes down during crisis times for these youth.

To illustrate, studies of parentally bereaved children and adolescents show unfortunate links between loss of a parent and a predisposition to certain diseases, a susceptibility to depression, poor school performance, delinquency, suicide attempts in adult life, and negative shifts in self-concept. Death of a parent or sibling increases the risk of an early adolescent experiencing psychological difficulties (*Bereavement* 1984, pp. 112–126).

Trouble with father

Though the variables just mentioned are upsetting to youth, an even more sensitive nerve is touched by the statement "I have trouble getting along with my father." Surprising as it may seem to armchair psychologists, difficulties with father are twelve times as likely to predict family disunity as the fact of divorce. A boy who is at odds with his dad is powerfully affected by his conflict situation and prone to condemn himself for it. His self-esteem goes down. Though such a young person is often less religious than are other church youth, the differences are not commensurate with the marked contrasts in how he feels about his family and about himself. Not to get along with dad is an emotionally potent variable. If there is conflict, therefore, someone is needed to take dad's place and provide psychological support.

What if the young person has trouble getting along with his or her mother? A separate analysis of such youth gives almost identical results, except for one addition. An inability to communicate is felt more keenly when mother lacks interest or will not listen. Such an impasse in communication is reported more often by youth who have trouble getting along with their mothers.

Here are some of the most sensitive and frustrating irritations being experienced by youth who have trouble getting along with either parent:

My parents (mother or father) nag me.
My parents (mother or father) try to pry into my private life.
My parents (mother or father) do not like some of my friends.

There is nothing in our survey that suggests a reason for the parent-youth conflict. Nowhere in any of the items of behavior, values, attitudes, or beliefs is there evidence that the youth themselves are posing obstacles to communication. The task appears to be one of moving *parents* closer to their children. The size of the task is indicated by the fact that one in four reports trouble getting along with the father. Of these, nearly half (44 percent) are also at odds with the mother.

Distress over Parental Relationships

Whereas the first characteristic identifies family pressures, the second describes the young person's feelings about parental relationships. It includes distress over lack of communication and understanding between a youth and his or her parents, chagrin over feeling treated like a child, and disappointment in his or her parents' distrust or rejection of him or her and his or her friends.

Lack of understanding

The cluster of items forming this characteristic describes parental attitudes and actions that interfere with understanding. From youth's answers to these items one can draw several conclusions. One-third of church youth are much bothered by their inability to communicate with mother. They find that the frequently used stratagem of either parent is to nag, criticize friends, express suspicions, and give orders. Parents of these youth display a notable lack of understanding and sensitivity about their teenager's feelings. Instead of communicating as one who respects another, they are inclined to do what destroys relationships. They dig into their child's privacy, as though suspecting the worst, and overcontrol his or her actions as though the teenager could not be trusted to act responsibly.

By comparison with the teachers and "experts" whom they meet, young people see their parents' way of treating them as ill-informed and ridiculous. Many teenagers doubt their parents' reliability and in some cases question their ability to rear children. Parenthood as a "natural right" may be seen as the last stand of the amateur in American society. This tongue-in-cheek comment applies especially to youth who suffer under conditions of poor family health, who live with parents not able to cope with life's realities—parents who in many instances can be called "living disasters." In many cases they are parents who, out of a mistaken concept of their role, are overstrict and distrustful.

Blocked communication between parents and youth typifies more homes than do shouting matches. It is frequently found in homes where parents are conscientious to a fault but inhibited by a mistaken concept of role. Instead of admitting their humanity and acknowledging their clay feet, they pose as authorities, godlike towers of strength and unfailing judgment. The message that comes through is "I'm okay, but you are not." The reaction of some youth is "hypocrite."

Too-strict parents

Overregulation of children is a common error of church people. When we divided the sample into groups based on youth's answer to the item "My parents (mother or father) are too strict," we found considerable variation, with about two out of five (39 percent) bothered very much or quite a bit by overstrictness.

A major irritant in the overstrict home has to do with communication. According to the youth reports, there is little discussion of problems and only telling by the parents. The typical too-strict parent nags and pries and is unwilling to credit youth with the sense to make their own decisions. Teenagers, they assume, must be told what to do.

A second source of distress is the way a too-strict parent relates to his or her children's friends. The stricter the parent, the less likely he or she is to approve of the friends his or her child enjoys. Over half (58 percent) of the youth of the strictest parents report that their friends are neither liked nor approved. They are mystified by their parents' behavior and can't understand why they act as they do. It is as though their parents have forgotten how it feels to be young.

One outcome of extreme strictness is greater tension in the home. No other groups under comparison contrast as sharply in parent-youth relationships as those divided on the basis of parental strictness. Extreme differences in scores appear on measures of family unity and parental understanding.

What happens to the young person? Self-regard tends to be low and self-condemnation high for youth who struggle under the regime of overcontrol. Mingled with these feelings is a longing to get out from under the parental thumb. One-half of overcontrolled youth say that a goal of personal freedom and independence is of "extreme importance" to them.

Another obvious outcome is parent-youth conflict. Life in the home becomes a power struggle—the two members cannot get along because each tries to assert his or her will over the other. Irritations increase for youth who feel saddled with tyrannical or overcontrolling parents, as shown in figure 3.

It should not be inferred from these comments that the ideal family should operate without controls. Permissiveness may be as ineffective as authoritarian methods. It is under conditions of either extreme that adolescents are most likely to rebel.

This became apparent in our 1984 study, Young Adolescents and Their Parents. We divided our sample of adolescents on the basis of their parents' style of control: authoritarian, permissive, or authoritative (democratic). Adolescents raised under an overly strict, authoritarian approach to parenting were more likely to reject traditional moral standards, become involved in acts of rebellion, and reject a personal faith. Likewise adolescents raised under a permissive parenting approach were more likely to become involved in hedonistic activities, reject authority, and disassociate themselves from the church. In contrast adolescents given authoritative and firm guidelines coupled with increasing freedom to make their own decisions were more likely to reflect high self-esteem, embrace the Christian faith, and become involved in serving activities.

The adolescent needs to be treated as a maturing person—one his or her parents speaks *with* rather than *to*. He or she needs a parent who is consistent and firm in discipline while remembering what adolescence was like. Trust is the essential element, a two-way street that must involve the child as well as the parent.

Figure 3. How Irritation with Parents Varies in Relation to Degree
Parents Are Perceived as Strict

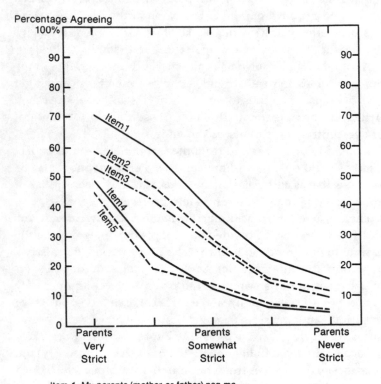

Item 1. My parents (mother or father) nag me.
Item 2. My parents seem to have forgotten how it feels to be young.
Item 3. My parents (mother or father) do not understand my dating problems.
Item 4. My parents (mother or father) do not let me make my own decisions.
Item 5. My parents (mother or father) try to pry into my private life.

Distrustful parents

Some parents hold the pessimistic view that the full bloom of original sin occurs in the teen years. In paranoid fashion they believe that devilment is afoot, requiring alertness for possible chicaneries. Distrustful and authoritarian parents of this kind impede good parental relationships. Kandel, in his 1972 study of youth in two worlds (the United States and Denmark), demonstrates that authoritarian parents are likely to be out of touch with their children. Their heavy emphasis on rules and obedience discourages open communication.

Similar findings were reported by Posterski in a 1984 study of 3,600 randomly selected Canadian high-school youth. He found lowest enjoyment of family life among teenagers raised in religiously authoritarian homes. Though a director of Intervarsity Christian Fellowship and thus heavily involved in Christian youth activities, he felt compelled by his data to present the hard news that "conservative-style religion is potentially detrimental to the enjoyment of parent-teen relationships" (Posterski 1985, pp. 15–19). Posterski identified conservative religion with a heavily moralistic and law-oriented interpretation of Christianity.

Feelings of mistrust are a potent factor in family conflict. When there is concern over parental distrust *it is nineteen times more likely to predict family disunity than the simple fact of a divorce.*

Distrustful parents are guilty of nagging, not approving of friends, imposing decisions, prying, being too strict, and pressing religion on their children. They do little to encourage the kind of democracy in which the whole family participates in decision making or where the children assist in working out rules. On the contrary, they tend to give orders with no attitude of caring.

Our data shows that distrustful parents sometimes have reason to be concerned about their children. Untrusted youth often act in ways that cause their parents to trust them even less. These people are more susceptible to group pressures concerning ethical decisions. Fewer believe in a personal God or consider a religious faith important. More are likely to get high on alcohol or to have sexual intercourse on a date. It is difficult to tell whether parents sense an inclination toward unacceptable behavior and become distrustful or whether the youth, sensing distrust, make deliberate decisions to justify their parents' suspicions. Whether parental distrust or rebellious behavior comes first, it is reasonable to say that distrust is a snowball rolling downhill, getting bigger and dirtier as it goes.

Sorenson's 1973 study, *Adolescent Sexuality in Contemporary America*, adds a helpful dimension. He reports that of all the sexual-behavior groups he studied, sexual adventurers are most in conflict with their parents. Of all sexual adventurers, 58 percent feel they have never gotten to know their fathers, and 40 percent believe they have never gotten to know their mothers.

One tragic response to a lack of parental trust is suicide. The percentage who consider self-destruction mounts in direct relation to a youth's feeling of being distrusted. Our data shows that, of the distrusted, more have the feeling they will not live long. Fewer see life as exciting, and fewer are hopeful for the future. Self-regard is lowest for youth who feel least trusted by their parents.

Family Disunity

A third characteristic of youth living in troubled homes is their sensitivity to a lack of closeness and oneness of family members. They are bothered by the frigid atmosphere and lack of understanding and consideration for one another; they are disturbed by the poor quality of interaction between parents and children.

Youth idealize a happy family. They often wish the family would enjoy social activities or sports or outings as a family, hoping these events would help bring everyone together.

In the more distressful family situations the youth are perplexed as well as troubled. They cannot understand why their parents act as they do, why father and mother do not get along as they should, why neither parent shows the interest a young person wants.

Predictors of family disunity

What contributes most to family disunity? What variables are most frequently associated with a tense emotional climate? What are the relative effects on family climate of such variables as parents' occupations, financial duress, illness, divorce, mobility, and the like? How important are variables about which something can be done—those affected by efforts such as open communication, conflict resolution, trust, right use of authority, and relating to one another?

To find answers we assessed the degree to which each of thirty-nine variables is related to family disunity. By means of a multivariate analysis we identified the irritations most frequently associated with distressed families.

I find it highly significant that sociological variables often cited as reasons for the "breakdown of the home" are of little importance. Matters such as socioeconomic level, mother's employment, mobility, or size of family are so minimal in their impact that they can be dismissed from consideration as far as the families of church youth are concerned.

What do emerge in the youth's self-reports are psychological issues. The one that most strongly predicts family disunity is the simple statement "My father and mother do not get along. This bothers me." *It is at least twenty times more powerful a predictor of family disunity than the fact of divorce.*[1] When parents are at odds with each other, youth are most likely to report a fractured or disunited home. This is far and away the most decisive variable in identifying a family that is bleeding and youth who are hurting. Ranking second in predictive power is parental distrust. Unless the parents are helped to make peace with each other and to learn what it means to trust, the children will suffer.

Admittedly comparing parental conflict with divorce is like comparing a high fever with death. One is a current situation, the other is past history. However, the comparison is valid in pointing up where remedial help is needed.

One boy wrote, "I hope [when married] that I will be stronger emotionally than my parents are. I hope not to fight and cry in front of my kids or be bitchy to them because of my own problems. Kids don't know what they have done when someone turns on them like that, and it hurts every time it happens— even at eighteen years old."

What account for the greatest variation in family unity are the issues to which the message and ministry of the Christian church addresses itself: the walls that separate people and alienate one person from another. These sources of dissension are ones about which something *can* be done.

Predictors of family unity

About half (53 percent) of the population of church youth report accord between their parents; the other half (47 percent) admit there are some differences. What makes for greater family unity? Our study singles out these three predictors: *parental accord, parental trust,* and *open communication.*

One in four youth report that their parents not only relate well to each other but also trust their teenage children. Most of these 25 percent have the added bonus of feeling free to discuss their problems with mother. Among the 16 percent who report the presence of all three positive qualities in their family life, few are in any way bothered by family disunity.[2]

Too Hurt to Help — Lack of Social Concern

A fourth characteristic of families in conflict is a lack of social concern among members. Troubled youth see their parents as unresponsive to the needs of people outside their home, uninvolved in any form of social action or helping activity.[3]

Most church youth report some social involvement by their families. Two out of three note that their parents care for others and believe their folks would rise to the defense of anyone being persecuted or hurt. They appreciate the example their parents set.

A large minority, however, do not see their parents as caring people. More than two in five (44 percent) admit that their families seldom do anything to help combat social problems and that they do not feel free to invite persons of other races into their homes. A similar percentage (42 percent) cannot recall any family conversations where they have discussed sharing their money with people in need.

As families become more and more preoccupied with their own conflicts and poor family health, they increasingly resist helping others. Parents who are at each other's throats can turn as quickly to fight racial integration or oppose new housing for senior citizens. The same embittered words that draw blood in the home can be used against others who threaten family security. Such parents should be encouraged to accept marriage counseling, for greater accord in the home and community and, most of all, for the psychological health of their children.

Suicide

Because suicide is so inextricably linked with low self-esteem and family conflict, it seems appropriate now to consider this third leading cause of death in the age group from fifteen to twenty-four years. Among persons of college age it is the second leading cause of death, outranked only by accidents. It marks the end of an unsuccessful struggle to tolerate frustration and despair, to achieve a sense of being, confidence in self, and confidence in being loved.

Among college students intellectual competence tends to characterize those who take their lives. A study by Bodin showed that suicides had higher grades than average (grade point averages of 3.18 as opposed to 2.50) and had won a greater proportion of scholastic awards (58 percent versus 5 percent). Yet they were filled with doubts about adequacy, dissatisfied with grades, and despondent over their general academic aptitude. It is likely that among the many factors are overambitious parents who push their children to achieve academically and to excel for the glory of the family.

Attempts to understand adolescent suicides began when Sigmund Freud called a meeting in 1910 to discuss the high rate of suicides among students. Since then various theorists have attempted to explain youthful suicides. Their theories, which group under three broad headings—sociological, psychological, and biological—reflect many variations. After reviewing these theories, Alan Berman and David Jobes concluded that "theory building in suicidology remains an open frontier" (Berman and Jobes, 1991, 51). Following are characteristics of adolescents who are suicidal or who have completed suicide.

1. *Psychiatric illness.* A 1986 study of a large number of completed suicides under the age of 30 showed that "psychiatric illness is a necessary but not sufficient condition of a suicide" (Rich et al, 1986).

2. *Substance abuse.* Suicide rates are triple for adolescent substance users over those of controls. Youth's "wish to die" increases dramatically after beginning substance use (Berman and Schwartz, 1990).

3. *Conduct disorder.* Apter found that conflict with police, shoplifting, drug selling and prostitution may outrank depression as a characteristic of suicidal persons (Apter et al, 1988).

4. *Social alienation.* Another behavioral characteristic of suicidal adolescents is social isolation (Farberou, 1989). They commonly report no close friends or close confidant.

5. *Influence of family.* Suicidal adolescents report poorer familial relationships, less affection, less enjoyable families and more negative views of their parents than typifies normal adolescents. Two factors are consistently associated with adolescent suicidal behavior: family stress and parental dysfunction (Pfeffer, 1989).

6. *Stressful life events.* Four areas most associated with suicide are concerns over achievement, family suicide, personal loss and

sexuality. Harry (1989) noted that homosexuals of both sexes are 2 to 6 times as likely to attempt suicide than are heterosexuals.

Of the many feeling states associated with suicidal behavior the most characteristic are feelings of human isolation and withdrawal. Conflicting home situations compound a youth's sense of isolation until it becomes intolerable. Stack, a research specialist on suicide, observes that families of teen suicide victims are more likely than other families to be characterized by recurrent yelling, less affection, a pattern of hostility, nagging parents, a relationship between parent and youth that permits no autonomy, and mothers who are depressed or dominant. Parents in such homes exercise either too much or too little discipline or neglect their children in favor of pursuing a career (Stack 1986).

From our sample we singled out 458 youth from the most troubled home situations. Nearly three in five (57 percent) of these youth say they sometimes consider suicide. (This is similar to the 62 percent of low self-esteem youth who admitted the same.) Conflict in one's home does indeed precipitate thoughts of death.

Differences between youth from troubled homes and all other youth are significant (see table 8). In the table we singled out those youth who scored in the top quartile of the scales for concern over family unity and parental pressures in 1970.

Table 8
Percentage of Youth Much Bothered by Thoughts of Death

	Percentage Much Bothered	
Item	Youth from Troubled Homes N = 458	All Other Youth N = 6,592
I sometimes think of dying or being killed	48%	27%
I get into moods where I can't seem to cheer up	35	13
Life is such a mess—sometimes I wish I could "get away from it all"	42	12

One wonders if the percentage of youth bothered by thoughts of suicide would be higher today. Some indication of an answer is available in the 1984 study of Catholic schools that serve low-income students. When asked how often they had thought about killing themselves in the previous year, three out of five students said never, leaving about 40 percent for whom this has been a consideration. In the 1990 study (*Effective Christian Education: A National Study of Protestant Congregations*) respondents were asked: "Has the thought of killing yourself come to you once or more times this past year?" A total of 44 percent of juniors and seniors said "yes" This percentage is well above the 27 percent of 7th and 8th graders who said "yes" (Benson and Eklin, 1990, 32). Significantly, more girls consider suicide than boys but more boys actually take their lives.

Lest the correlation between family ill health and low self-esteem be overemphasized, it should be noted that a large minority of youth whose families are in turmoil do not entertain thoughts of suicide. Many cope with their situations and rise above the stress. Likewise many who commit suicide come from loving, stable Christian homes. One should be concerned when an adolescent becomes withdrawn, careless of his or her appearance, unable to concentrate, disinterested in academic work, and apathetic and fatigued. These are some of the commonly observed symptoms of depression that precede suicide.

It is disturbing for some communities that a suicide seemingly can trigger others. This suggests that imitation may be a significant factor in causing suicides. A 1986 study by Stack correlated suicides for the years 1968 to 1980 with stories of suicides by celebrities and noncelebrities. Using accounts given national coverage during those years, he demonstrated that suicides of people ages fifteen to thirty-four increase when such stories appear. Though finding the correlation to be significant, he nonetheless concludes that imitation is no more than a secondary cause of suicide.

Suicide Prevention

The role of a religious faith is seldom mentioned in articles on preventing suicides. Stack found a significant and negative relationship between church attendance and suicide during the years 1954 and 1978. With rates of unemployment and military participation controlled, he found that suicide rates went down as church attendance went up. For the age groups of fifteen and twenty-nine, a 1 percent increase in church attendance was associated with a 1.4 percent decrease in suicide (Stack 1983, p. 247). For young females decline in church attendance was the most significant predictor of suicide.

In a later study he showed that two factors, religion and divorce in one's family, account for up to 90 percent of the variation in youth's suicide rate (Stack 1986). Because causality cannot be inferred from correlations such as these, we cannot conclude that lack of church attendance and parental divorce cause teen suicides. But we can assume that an important factor in suicide prevention is helping youth to become identified with a caring congregation and helping parents strengthen their marriage through seminars, counseling, and retreats.

Encouragement to think in this direction is also found in the 1990 study of 48,000 public school youth (grades 6–12) conducted by Search Institute. Only 10 percent of youth active in a religious institution reported having attempted suicide as compared to 17 percent of those inactive. Similar differences between the two groups of youth show for all at-risk behaviors (Eklin and Roehlkepartain, 1992).

Shneidman, who has over thirty-five years of experience as a clinical suicidologist, identified ten characteristics of suicide and the therapy task for each. Several of these provide an analogue for a ministry of prevention.

1. *Communication of intent.* Characteristically suicidal people give friends clear clues of their intention. Our task is to adopt a listening stance so that we can hear the chance remarks and deep concerns.

2. *Unbearable pain.* The pain the person is trying to escape through suicide is reduced when he or she is encouraged to talk about his or her frustration. Being listened to can be therapeutic.

3. *Hopelessness.* Because the underlying emotion for suicidal persons is hopelessness, the friend or therapist's task is to give a transfusion of hope. This fact underscores the impor-

tance of contacts and conversations that are hope inspiring.
4. *Seeking a solution through suicide.* To understand the drive toward suicide one needs to discover the problem the person is seeking to solve. Once the problem is discovered the task is to address the solution the person wishes were possible and to show that other options besides suicide are available.
5. *Constriction of options.* Characteristically the range of options narrows for a suicidal person until the mind panics and sees only two options: a magical solution or suicide. The need is to increase the person's awareness of other options or possibilities.
6. *Ambivalence.* A suicidal person wants to live and to die. It is important to stay in touch with the person so that one can reinforce the person's desire for life (Shneidman 1985).

These six characteristics of a suicidal person shows that a ministry of suicide prevention includes adopting a listening stance, maintaining contact, giving hope-filled responses, and bringing the person to someone who can give professional help. Such an approach is helpful for adolescents who are troubled over any issue or situation in life.

Has the Cry Changed?

During the first seven years (1970–77) since our original study we found no change. In fact, measures of personal understanding and family unity for church youth yielded identical scores for those years.

In 1980 slight changes did appear for Lutheran youth. More youth reported family pressures such as sickness, financial problems, divorce, and unemployment. This increase, though small, was one that could not be explained as due to chance factors. On the positive side fewer of these youth saw their parents lacking in social concerns. Hence one can say that for Lutheran youth the cry remained relatively unchanged from 1970 to 1980.

By 1985 one could expect the accelerated growth in single-parent families, the epidemic increase in divorce, and the new phenomenon of blended families to be showing their eroding effects on the quality of family life. One significant indicator of change in family life does appear in a ten-year comparison (1976–85) for high-school seniors. A significant increase in arguing or fighting with one or the other parent appears for this population (table 9). But one might expect a greater increase. It is here that the limitation of high-school seniors becomes apparent. It does not include dropouts, a disproportionate number of whom come from tragic or conflict-ridden family situations. The significance of not including dropouts is seen in these dramatic statistics: approximately 25 percent of all white youth, 40 percent of all black youth, and 50 percent of all Hispanic youth fail to graduate from high school (Hodgkinson 1986, p. 28). It is accurate to say, then, that a significant number of American youth are not included in the annual surveys of high-school seniors.

Table 9
Ten-Year Comparison of Seniors' Relationships with Parents

	Percentage Answering Yes		
Item	1976	1985	Percent Difference
Have argued or had a fight with either parent in the last 12 months			
3 or more times	22	24	2*
5 or more times	41	44	3*

*significant at .01 level

Changes among Church Youth

Church youth show a slight change, but not in the expected direction. Gupta's fifteen-year trend analysis (1970–85) shows a slight but statistically significant gain in the two available measures, family unity and parental understanding. Rather than showing family life to be deteriorating among families of church youth, the highly reliable measures show gains that cannot be accounted for by chance.[4]

Two explanations may be offered to account for these results. The sample may be a select sample, because families in trouble tend to drop out of the fellowship of a congregation. Fewer remain active when divorce, unwanted pregnancies, conflicts, or violence disrupt home and family. Hence the enhanced measures of family health may simply reflect that more of the youth are from intact families and that youth from troubled families are dropping out of congregational life in increasing numbers.

Another explanation has to do with the faith encouraged by a congregation. We have found that where an active evangelical, nonmoralistic faith characterizes a family, one is more apt to find close family life. It is possible that the increase we see in measures of family cohesiveness means that in 1985 more homes are taking religion seriously than did so in 1970. Congregations with such families may be the ones choosing to use the survey service in 1983 to 85. Both explanations are likely to be true.

In lieu of all that has been said, the question remains: Has the cry of the psychological orphan changed significantly for church youth? Our answer is no. The dynamics are the same as those identified in 1970 and the pecentage troubled with the cry remains largely the same for church youth. One can assume that one in five congregational youth is deeply troubled over parental relationships. One can assume also that a higher percentage of troubled youth characterizes those outside the fellowship of a congregation.

One would expect that these continuing shifts in family structure and dynamics over the last fifteen years would show their impact in a more significant way in our data on church youth. Evidence of the impact may be delayed. It is possible that five years from now greater changes in our measures will appear as more children raised in difficult home situations reach high-school age. This will be true only if troubled or stressed families continue in the fellowship of a congregation.

Toward Family Health

Changing parental attitudes is an appropriate goal for religious institutions, whose business is to change beliefs and values. Fortunately we know of ways to accomplish such changes. As parents are helped to love each other, to establish a climate of trust, and to begin communicating with their teenage children, a revolution ensues in the home. At least half the parents of church youth would profit from education to bring about such changes.

Our basic task is not to solve people's problems but to provide what is needed so that they can assume responsibility for their own situations. We can provide a point of view, information on family dynamics, viable options, a supportive environment, and a way to respond selectively to available options.

A Point of View

When we view the heartache one person can cause for another we discern the pervasive quality of man's sinfulness. It stimulates one's appetite to control, manipulate, and dominate people. Its fruit is a hardness of heart that is especially devastating in the close confines of a family.

Paradoxically, though one's family shapes (some people would say "determines") his or her behavior, God holds every person responsible for his or her actions. Scripture makes this abundantly clear and for good reason. All of us, parents and youth alike, are adept at buckpassing; it began with Adam blaming Eve. We prefer to blame our wrongdoings on the failures and sins of others and in so doing run away from responsibility.

One who relates to troubled youth should be clear on this: Each person is responsible for his or her actions. No one should be allowed to excuse his or her irresponsibility on the grounds that it was caused by others' treatment of him or her.

Each person in a troubled home has the possibility of changing his or her response to the situation. Though powerfully influenced, he or she is still free to act. How a young person has been treated limits his or her options, but does not determine his or her response. Though determinism is the basic fabric of the physical universe, choice within a limited framework is the fact of human existence.

Changing Family Dynamics

The changing nature of the family is reflected in the statistics. In 1955, 60 percent of the households in the United States consisted of a working father, a housewife mother, and two or more children of school age. By 1985 that kind of family unit had dropped from 60 percent to 7 percent, an astonishing shift (Hodgkinson 1986). The United States Bureau of the Census tells us that 59 percent of children born in 1983 will, before reaching age eighteen, live a period of time with only one parent. Here is the breakdown:

12 percent born out of wedlock
40 percent born to parents who divorce
5 percent born to parents who separate
2 percent born to parents who will die
___
59 percent

In other words, only 41 percent of the youth we work with will reach age eighteen having lived in a two-parent family.

Oxford Analytica, in the book *America in Perspective* (1986) has the following to say about American families of the future: "Americans will live longer, but their marriages will not. Family life will become even more fragile and less predictable than in the past. But Americans will keep on trying again in remarriage. More will avoid marriage and more will live together without marriage. The majority will end their childbearing days decisively through sterilization" (p. 11).

One of the most significant changes in family composition since 1970 has been the substantial growth in the number of single-parent families. In the Minneapolis public school system, for instance, 48 percent of the children in the school year 1983–84 were from single-parent homes. Ninety percent of the time the single parent is a mother who has to be both father and mother. Many divorced parents, however, remarry, and new families are formed. In fact 45 percent of all marriages in 1983 were remarriages (Oxford Analytica 1986, p. 87). It is predicted that such newly formed stepfamilies will be the norm by the year 2000.

But the art of blending divided families is only the first step toward recovery of a strong family. Potentially divisive dynamics characterize blended families. These must be understood and handled *before a strong family can emerge.*

Search Institute made a 1986 study of the following family situations: stepfamilies, single-parent families, and adoptive homes. When these samples of several hundred youths were each compared to youth living in nuclear families, striking contrasts appeared on a number of measures,[5] as indicated below.

1. More adolescents in stepfamilies consistently evidenced deviant behavior, erotic activities, parent-youth conflict, and identity and achievement problems. More of these youth also felt they received less parental affection, less nurturance, and more authoritarian or permissive treatment.

2. When the sample of 302 adolescents who were adopted in infancy by both parents was compared with the sample of 5,059 peers raised in nuclear families, the adopted adolescents showed a lower achievement motivation; were viewed by their mothers as not doing their best in school; tended to get into trouble; talked back to adults; did not respect parental values; and were rebellious. The self-reports of these adolescents, when compared with their 5,059 peers, showed greater conflict with their parents; greater desire for autonomy; more involvement in clandestine behavior; more anger; and more feeling that their parents were too strict and

not trusting. More adoptive than nonadoptive mothers admitted they nagged, found their child difficult to understand, and viewed parenting as difficult.

3. Adolescents in single-parent homes gave responses most like adolescents in nuclear families. However, a separate study in 1984, comparing 482 single parents with parents of intact families, showed the stress that single parents feel. More are unhappy about their family life, worry about finances, and view their children as hard to handle and not doing well in school (Strommen and Strommen 1985).

Addressing family issues such as these is not part of the church's tradition, nor has it been an ingredient in programs of Christian education. Therefore, changes are required: (1) changes in attitudes toward people whose behavior is puzzling or disappointing; (2) changes in congregational programs to accommodate the questions and needs in new family situations; and (3) changes by church members resulting in a caring outreach to people who now absent themselves from the church's fellowship. Our data clearly show that when a divorce or unwanted pregnancy occurs the parents involved drop out of congregational life. And tragically these parents and their children are the very ones who especially need the support and care of a congregation.

Clearly the implication is that a ministry to children and youth must include a ministry to parents. How parents handle the dynamics of single parenthood, of blended families, or of various kinds of stress powerfully affects their children's response to the gospel. Needed are classes for youth and parents in how to improve the way they relate to each other, how to create close family life, how to communicate with each other, and, above all, how to share faith and pray with one another.

Needed also is an awareness that "business as usual is no longer possible" in youth and family ministries. A clear mandate of this chapter is outreach to parents and families inclined to drift away from their congregation when they experience difficulties as a family. Lest the church be seen as a place primarily for people who have "made it," the mandate is clear: Reach out to the troubled parent and troubled youth to help them to find the healing, redemptive love of Christ through his followers.

Viable Options

Our task is to make hope-inspiring contacts with troubled youth and parents, to make them aware of their options, and then to help them make a choice and commitment. By responding selectively each person can allow into his or her life what he or she knows will change him or her.

One dynamic force that is seldom understood is the life-changing awareness of God's forgiveness. This is one of the possibilities that troubled families need to discover.

Another option focuses upon some kind of educational experience that translates large theological concepts into everyday language and application. One such educational program, called Peer Counselor Training, uses a sequence of classes to train parents in reflection, active listening, responding to a child, and resolving conflicts.[6] Another is Parent Effectiveness Training, developed by Thomas Gordon.[7] Convinced that most parents sincerely want to raise emotionally healthy children but lack the insight and skills to do so, Gordon has developed a systematic program of training for the job of parenthood. It has proved effective in modifying parent-child relationships; parents often need not therapy but education about human relationships.

Support Groups

In *Habits of the Heart* author Robert Bellah draws an upsetting picture of Americans as increasingly self-centered and isolated from society, without the capacity to enter into deep, lasting relationships. The major moral dilemmas this fierce individualism poses for our society center on people's growing inability or unwillingness to make commitments (Bellah et al. 1985). His description applies to youth and parents, many of whom belong to a "family of strangers." They need a group that gives them the feeling of being uniquely valued; in other words, the support that is unavailable in their own families.

Adults who work with youth in a church setting must give increasing emphasis to the "nonkindred family" made up of friends. Young people who do not have a kindred family need a church fellowship that provides the experience of communicating in depth and the security of people with whom they can identify. The church of Jesus Christ has a history, a tradition, a people, and a way of life that can become the only "family" some youth will experience.

That a family approach can make a unique contribution to a program of Christian education is being recognized and applied in many places. Note what one of my reviewers penned on the side of her manuscript: "We have started a family Sunday school class at home with three families because our children object to the 'school' approach on Sunday morning. We have a class of eighteen ranging in age from four to forty-five."

The benefits of "nonkindred families" are real and measurable. In a large research study called Youth Reaching Youth we found that group-oriented programs that taught friendship skills also developed support groups that served as "family" experiences.[8] At the end of seventeen months of weekly meetings (with appropriate control groups) the following changes were recorded:

1. Self-esteem increased dramatically, and self-criticism and personal anxiety decreased.
2. The youth increased measurably in their openness to people and ideas; they learned to share themselves with parents and to be more self-disclosing with their pastors.[9]

4. Cry of Social Concern

I can sit down and think about the world and the war, and I just cry.

An eighteen-year-old girl

Jeannie is intelligent, attractive, always busy in the way that bright high-school students tend to be, sparkling with enthusiasm, full of giggles and life at parties—a thoroughly charming girl. She is a leader in both her high school and her church youth group. Her college education is being financed by a fund her parents started before she was born. You would never guess that she has anything to be troubled about.

During her high-school career she cried out for help in a way no one noticed. She came into a meeting of youth-group officers one evening looking very thoughtful. That morning she had gone with a group from her high school to visit a home for the mentally retarded. She was silent during the early part of the meeting; then all at once, apropos of nothing, she said grimly, "I get so darned disgusted, sometimes, when we sit here and haggle about whether we want to invite the ninth graders in on our next party, and what we're going to do at the party, and all that kind of junk, when there are people living in old people's homes, and hospitals, and places for mentally retarded people who don't have anybody to care about them. And people are starving, and people are fighting . . . " She broke off, conscious that others were staring. "I just wish sometimes we did something that really mattered, that made a difference to people who need so much and who don't . . . " she trailed off lamely. After a pause the meeting got back on the rails and settled the necessary details for the party.

The voice of social conscience is not always loud and insistent. It will not always come on strong, like the boisterous brashness of a boy covering up his feeling of worthlessness or the stormy tears of the girl who longs for peace in her home. The signals of social concern that high-school students send require a special alertness. They may come subtly, infrequently, or perhaps in such an exaggerated form that the impulse is to laugh and forget them, or perhaps to refuse to allow them to be put into action through the church.

The concern may surface as a quiet question asked in private, following a sermon or program meant to stir the social conscience. It may show itself in a boy's withdrawing from the youth group and getting to work on a political campaign. It may be a request to talk privately or in group discussions about social issues—war, poverty, discrimination.

Our studies show that many of the socially concerned are solid humanists who do not believe in the gospel; as bright, well-adjusted, and sensitive people these change-oriented youth are some of the "unbelieving" critics of the church. An equal proportion of the youth described in this chapter, however, reflect a knowledge of the Christian faith and a love for their church.

Youth of both motivations are sufficiently bright, sophisticated, and mature to have grasped the message of the gospel and to hold it up against their church's track record on social action. Their expressions of that comparison may sound harsh, critical, and hard to take, but they are another way of sounding the cry.

The sensitive youth worker or parent will be alert to indications of concern. More than that, recognizing that the concern is often there but unexpressed, he or she will provide opportunities for expression. It is the clear message of our data that the concerns are there.

This chapter focuses on youth whose cries of anger over injustice became a cacophony during the years 1965 to 70. They can be distinguished by means of five major characteristics. These youth are (1) humanitarian, (2) oriented to change, (3) socially involved, (4) concerned over national issues, and (5) critical of the institutional church, in which adults seem not be "caring."

These characteristics of socially concerned youth do not change with the years. What changes is the number of youth who are socially concerned. In 1970 national issues and a concern for the welfare of others became a preoccupation for a sizable minority of church youth. By 1985 the number of concerned youth had eroded under the decaying influence of a self-centered value orientation. Though diminished in number socially concerned church youth in 1985 retain the same characteristics found in 1970.

In 1969 a cry of protest erupted on college campuses throughout the United States as students demanded an end to the war in Vietnam. By the spring of 1970 a majority of college students were opposed to fighting in any form, whether for the purpose of containing Communists, of maintaining a position of power in the world, or of upholding our honor as a first-rate power. For them the compelling cause in life was social justice. Wrongs being done to people had to be righted, and these students were of a mind to bring about needed changes without further delays.

Though a majority of the college youth rejected the philosophy of violence, many employed acts of violence as the only means strong enough to gain their ends. Most students resisted the tactics of radical activists but sympathized with their goals. High-school students too were antiwar and concerned over what was happening in their world. A large number were sympathetic to the protest movement and many joined the parades and mass demonstrations.

During this historic period leaders of time-honored institutions like churches and schools cast worried glances toward the future. In discussion I found a group of leading Minneapolis businessmen preoccupied with student attacks on big business and fearful that student reaction would roll like a tidal wave into their future and adversely affect the economy of the country.

Our research team, interviewing college and seminary presidents, denominational administrators, and church educators and leaders in preparation for Search Institute's *Study of Generations,* met these same fears for the future. Will today's youth remain within the institutional church? Will they, as tomorrow's leaders, support established congregations? Nothing was voiced more often in the interviews than concern over what was happening among students and youth.

Meanwhile the mass media, assuming this to be its legitimate news function, played up the violence, destruction of property, and confrontations. The inevitable result was a general loss of perspective. Many students joined causes they did not understand, taking part as if protests were a new form of fun and games. Their antics, usually featured by the media, infuriated segments of the public. Sharp polarization began to be apparent.

By the spring of 1970 student provocations that had dominated the news for many months had awakened a slumbering grizzly bear of public reaction. Understanding and sympathy for student causes shifted to anger and resentment. Adults who had looked indulgently on the antics of young idealists of the "now generation" began to refer to "troublemakers and spoiled brats." A crescendo of angry voices demanded cutbacks in student subsidies and an end to one-sided demands and simplistic prescriptions for instant change.

The high watermark in youth's unrest and rebellion came at Kent State University on May 4, 1970, when an order to fire on antiwar demonstrators left four young people dead and nine wounded. This tragedy and its aftermath brought to a point of high visibility the polarization of opinion and feeling that had been gathering through the spring. Many of the older generation approved the order to fire as a necessary step toward restoring law and order, deplorable though the consequences were. Dramatizing this same belief that authority *must* be asserted and order restored, on May 8, 1970, a group of construction workers on New York's Wall Street disrupted a parade of antiwar demonstrators and manhandled some of the young demonstrators.

Students, on the other hand, reacted to the Kent State "massacre" with horror and anger. On May 10, 448 universities and college were either closed or on strike. The spirit of protest also involved many high schools, some of which experienced protest walkouts and teach-ins with many students participating.

Characteristics of Socially Concerned Youth

May 1970, a high point in the radical political action that had been mounting through the sixties, was the time during which our survey was taken. One can expect that our survey data would reflect youth's feelings about social injustice. A cry of anger, disappointment, and sometimes outrage has been and always will be heard within the church. It is the cry of the peacemakers, the merciful, the friends of outcasts. It comes from those who are pained by the sufferings of others and unable to tolerate a status quo that does little to alter the lot of needy people.

We singled out 335 socially concerned youth with characteristics like those shown in figure 4.[1] Then we compared them with all others, using 420 items from the survey to determine where they resemble all other church youth and where they are distinctly different.

In general they identify with the sufferings of people more than do other church youth. They are inwardly pained when they see minorities abused, they worry about world starvation, and they are troubled when they see people in need. They want to become involved in effecting changes that will push the realities of life closer to the oft-repeated ideals of church and government.

Socially concerned youth tend to be bright, with many more drawing above-average grades then do typical church youth in general. More of them have parents who are in a profession or have a college or graduate-school background.

They say they take time to think through why they believe and act as they do, and more say their beliefs and values have changed in the past year or so. What these changes are cannot be learned from this survey, but they appear to be in values and in their concept of what is important in life. To questions of doctrinal beliefs, religious practices, and involvement in the life of the congregation socially concerned youth answer as do all church youth.

In ranking a variety of life values more of the socially concerned list money as of "least importance"; physical appearance or attractiveness gets a low billing for nearly half these youth. A large number credit meaningful work with "extreme importance," and the majority insist that a person should look out not only for himself of herself but also for the welfare of others. These values and beliefs are associated with their heightened sensitivity to the needs of others. One illustration is in the area of race relations. Many more in this socially concerned group than in other groups see themselves as more liberal in their opinions than their parents.

Feeling for People

As indicated by figure 4, a strong characteristic of socially concerned and involved youth is their humanitarian attitude and feeling for people who are commonly condemned. This attitude reflects the presence of an open-mindedness, sensitivity, and compassion toward those who are often criticized and judged harshly; blacks, Jews, people of enemy countries, Communists, and the like. The responses of socially concerned youth imply an understanding of the essential equality of all men before God.

A quality that shines through the self-report of these youth is mercy. They reject almost unanimously a punitive attitude toward enemy countries, the denial of food for Communists, or unusual punishment for sex killers. In these matters a much higher percentage than typifies church youth generally reflect a merciful attitude. Part of the difference may be found in their concept of God. For instance, almost unanimously they refuse to believe that mental illness is a punishment that God sends for certain sins.

Though most church youth do not countenance the idea of excluding blacks or other racial groups from church or nonchurch activities, the socially concerned are almost unanimous in their rejection of such tactics. Though a few falter when the issue narrows to having a person of another race for a next-door neigh-

Figure 4. Characteristics of Socially Concerned Youth

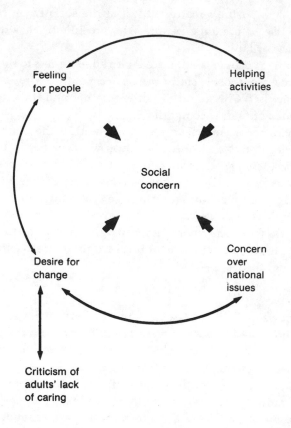

Heaviness of arrow indicates strength of intercorrelation.

bor, a majority agree they would not mind. Again, a majority believe their families are open to accepting persons of other races into their neighborhood.

Discernment and clarity of conviction are other qualities that can be attached to the socially concerned youth. They are far more likely to discern and reject an anti-Semitic remark than the large population of church youth; they largely reject the notion that Jews are less ethical than others and that Jews are more likely to cheat in business matters. Most of the socially concerned youth refuse to prejudge people who are identified with the Jewish race or faith.

Openness to people is associated with an openness to the findings of science. Most socially concerned youth do not believe that science and Christianity fight each other and therefore reject the idea of their incompatibility.

The evidence seems clear. One finds within the church extremely perceptive and sensitive youth who cry out in protest over the way some people are being treated. They associate their convictions with Christianity, being convinced that the elimination of all racial discrimination is a goal of Christianity. Their sensitivities also deter them from agreeing with commonly heard criticism of the poor; they resist the assertion that most poor people could alter their lot if they only took advantage of their opportunities.

Desire for Change

To some people a liberal is a bad guy, a conservative, a good guy. Those who think this way always have difficulty with the person of Christ, who in many ways was a liberal and a revolutionary and whose disciples were said to be "turning the world upside down."

Socially concerned youth are more liberal in their approach to life and more ready to break with traditions. This may mean radical changes or a nostalgic return to the past. From our data we learn what changes they especially want. Among two hundred possibilities we find that six items draw a heightened response from the socially concerned: the war, military service, the unlikelihood of peace, an unresponsive government, social injustice, and the chasm between professed ideals and the realities of everyday life.

The shock that these youth feel as they reach their teen years is described in this young person's statement:

> In the American education system, each child receives the impression that America is a great, strong, nearly infallible country. America is the magic land of opportunity where Cinderellas and Horatio Algers run rampant, where God is always on our side, where every wrong is righted with blind yet merciful justice. What a shock it is for the child later to realize that America does have corrupt legislators, unfair laws, apathetic citizens. How horrible to discover that America was not always on "the right side" in foreign affairs in the past and is not now; to see that its foreign aid policies and programs are motivated at least as much by ultimate financial and political gains as by altruism. (Sabine 1971, p. 120)

Because the tragedy of war troubles these youth most, one can expect opposition to militarism. Most assert that war is basically wrong and that a citizen should have the right to decide in which wars he or she will fight. Here they part company with a large segment of other church youth.

As would be expected, the socially concerned are generally ready to support legislation that provides free medical care and adequate housing for everyone, irrespective of their ability to pay. Another example of their people-oriented stance is their quite unanimous rejection of the statement "It is wrong to date a person of another race." They also disagree that people of any color have the right to keep others out of their neighborhood. Here the socially concerned have strong support from all other church youth because three-fourths of them join in disagreeing with that statement.

Helping Activities

A sign of growing maturity is the ability to feel for individuals other than oneself, for groups other than one's own. Socially involved youth show this maturity of spirit in their sensitivity to abused minorities. They suffer over the thought of starving people and are distressed when they observe their peers headed for tragedy. Less troubling is the knowledge that someone else does not have a personal faith, although only a fourth of our sample show no concern over their friends' lack of faith.

There are many ways of expressing concern for others and varying motivations for being helpful. In this study social action is positively linked to social concern and religious commitment. Some are driven to action by sensitivity to world problems, others by gratitude for a personal faith. Both motivations characterize the majority of socially concerned youth.

Some heart-warming stories can be told of socially involved youth working as volunteers in communities, churches, social agencies, or hospitals. While serving they are also learning. Because of the educative value of social involvement, public schools are making community service a curricular activity. They have found, for instance, that cross-age tutoring where older students assist younger ones, is valuable for all concerned. Service not only builds self-esteem, enhances social skills and increases leadership skills, but it also encourages a value orientation. Note, for instance, the contrasts in values between youth actively involved in service and those not involved. This comparison is based on a 1992 study of 33,000 9th-12th graders, where youth who serve one hour or more a week are compared with those who spend no time serving (Eklin and Roehlpartain, 1992).

Table 10
Values of Servers vs. Non-Servers

Value	Servers	Non-Servers
1. Values helping people	68%	31%
2. Is involved in church or synagogue	74	38
3. Is concerned about world hunger	60	29
4. Values sexual restraint	47	27
5. Is motivated to achieve in school	82	60

Concern over National Issues

Youth's concerns over national issues reflect the issues most troubling to them or those given the most media attention during a given year. In 1970, the top concern of church youth was the fear this country would be destroyed. The future appeared to them to promise more violence, revolution, and eventually total destruction of this country. Though the word *Armageddon* was not familiar, world destruction stood as a frightening prospect for many.

By 1988 this fear of annihilation by a nuclear war had subsided. For high school seniors the crime and violence in our country had become a top concern. Ranking close second among 11 social problems was the issue of drug abuse. These two social issues worried four of five seniors either "sometimes" or "often". (Bachman et al, 1991, pp 180–181).

A shift in youth's concerns can be seen in the 11,000 letters written to members of Congress by 7th and 8th grade students across the United States in 1992. The concern they referred to most often in their letters was drug and alcohol abuse. Ranking a close second was their worry over what is happening to the environment.

Interestingly, a new concern emerged in their letters, namely, the troubling issue of teenage pregnancies. When writing to their Congress persons these 7th and 8th graders identified this concern almost as many times as the two mentioned first (Youth Update, 1992).

It is quite clear that youth's concerns over national issues vary over periods of time.

On the average, four out of five church youth expressed some degree of concern over all eleven of the national issues listed. Though it was a small group that cried out in protest, a majority of church youth were concerned.

Criticism of Adult Caring

Youth most distressed over social ills also expressed the greatest disappointment in their church. As social consciousness heightened, criticism of the church mounted. But not the facile criticisms of intellectual roughnecks who rushed onto the national scene like gangbusters. Most of the socially concerned young people described in this chapter had deep attachments to their congregations and reflected attitudes similar to other church youth. It was at church that they met their best friends and saw adults whom they knew. Four out of five were likely to hear their names called out by some adult when attending a service. Most of them acknowledged the kindness of many adults and appreciated that they were quick to help the sick or needy. They agreed, too, that church teaching had much to say about life as it really is. Yet they were disappointed in their church.

About half felt that adults (1) seriously consider doing something about current social problems; (2) are concerned about world starvation, war, poverty; (3) seek ways to respond more meaningfully to human needs; (4) are interested in the youth; and (5) make young people feel welcome at a service. The other half did not agree or were not sure where the adults stood.

The critique gained a majority when it focused on what the congregation failed to do as a corporate group; socially concerned youth did not want to "follow the example of my congregation in its stand on social problems." They were convinced that most adults in their congregation would not "be able to tell you what the purpose of our church is."

The unpleasant fact is that many socially concerned youth did not believe their church would accept a family of another race into their community or welcome people who look different (richer, poorer, another race, different in hair or dress). Many did not think their church was doing anything about problems of social concern (e.g., housing, racism, injustice, civil rights) or trying to improve parent-youth relationships. Though they saw individual concern, they felt it was not expressed *organizationally* by the congregation.

Example is a powerful educational tool, both for negative as well as positive teaching. Most of these youth, though aware of the goodwill and sincerity of individual members, looked with dismay at the little their congregations were doing. They may have prejudged the church as adults are prone to prejudge youth. Sometimes, of course, their dismay was due to lack of *knowing* what was being done.

But their critique cannot be dismissed as mere reflections of unhappy people; if negativism were involved, it would show in other ways as well. Neither can it be dismissed as the voice of outsiders. These young people were altruistic and solid members of their congregations. The cause of offense was more likely the unresponsiveness of congregations to deep and immediate needs or perhaps youth's ignorance of what was actually being done.

It has not been the habit of adults to listen seriously to youth. Listening comes hardest when youth are critical of adult action, particularly when adults already feel guilt about their inaction. Yet that painful listening must be done.

Proportion of Youth Who Are Socially Concerned

It is difficult to estimate the number of church youth who were socially concerned in 1970; a precise answer requires that we use as criteria all the characteristics given in this chapter. When the ecumenical sample was divided using the three strongest predictors of a humanitarian attitude, we gained the following rough estimate:

Fifty-four percent thought about why they believed and acted as they did. (They scored above average in humanitarian attitudes.)

Thirty-two percent did as indicated above *and* achieved excellent or above average grades. (They scored higher on humanitarian attitudes.)

Nine percent did as indicated on the above criteria *and* were strongly oriented to change. (They scored highest on humanitarian attitudes.)

On this basis one can conclude that one in ten youth in 1970 was a militant for change. Surrounding them was a larger group that, though less eager for change, was sensitive to and concerned about social injustice. Combined, the groups did account for one-third of church youth. In 1985 the proportion was closer to one-fifth. The same was true for girls (9th–12th grade) in 1990, but only for one-tenth of the boys (Benson and Eklin, 1990, 34).

Has the Cry Changed?

Yes, indeed, and strikingly so. Today, with the collapse of communism and the dissolution of the former Soviet Union, the threat of a nuclear war has all but disappeared. The two superpowers formerly poised to pull the trigger on each other are now involved in dismantling their nuclear missiles. The cry indeed has changed. The focus of concern has shifted to internal problems. This is well-illustrated in the list presented in letter form to members of Congress by junior high youth in 1992. The concerns mentioned most often in their letters are given below in the order of frequency mentioned.

1. Drug and alcohol abuse
2. Environment
3. Teenage pregnancy
4. Education
5. AIDS
6. Homelessness
7. Gun control
8. Child abuse
9. Suicide, depression
10. Gang violence
(Youth Update, 1992)

These issues are associated with a growing national problem—adolescents at risk. This phrase is one being used to describe youth involved in behaviors that can sabotage their future, compromise their well-being. While many adolescents do survive departures from desirable behavior, a significant and growing percentage of American youth are burdened with lifetime scars. Joy Dreyfoos, who made a national evaluation of programs that address youth behaviors, estimates that we face the "potential loss of fully one-fourth of today's youth. They will never become productive citizens unless given immediate attention" (Dryfoos, 1989, vi). It is evident that young people, seeing what is happening to their peers, share in this concern.

A dominating concern of high-school students in the mideighties was the possibility of nuclear war. Striking evidence of this appeared in the 1984 study of Catholic schools serving low-income families. When asked, "How likely do you think it is that a major nuclear war will occur in your lifetime?" those answering "very likely" or "quite likely" included 36 percent of ninth graders and 30 percent of twelfth graders. When asked, "How much do you worry about the possibility of nuclear war?" even greater numbers, answered "very likely" or "quite likely"—49 percent of ninth graders and 36 percent of twelfth graders. Interestingly the degree of worry varied by race, with Hispanics showing highest concern (55 percent), blacks next highest (49 percent), and whites the lowest (35 percent). These racial differences in concern over this world issue were striking.

More significant than this shift in focus, however, was youth's shift in *motivation.* Beginning with the year 1965, often identified as a watershed year, youth's values began a quiet shift toward greater emphasis on individualism, personal freedom, and tolerance for diversity, a trend that found full expression in the seventies. The shift was away from traditional moral beliefs to a value orientation that stressed "doing your own thing" or "letting instincts be your guide." The new accent was on making choices with the pronoun *I* paramount. Concern for oneself came to overrule concern for others. Accompanying this greater preoccupation with self came alarming changes in behavior: hedonistic lifestyles, less willingness to make commitments, and a lessening of loyalty to institutions. Advocates of this value orientation were many. An example was Robert Ringer in his bestseller *Looking Out for Number One.* Here the author advocated weighing every human transaction on the scale of self-interest—if the balance tips to one's own personal happiness, do it.

This shift in motivation had an eroding effect on universal moral principles such as honesty, restraint, keeping promises, and personal integrity. A classic illustration is seen in the attitudes of high-school seniors toward cheating on a test. When asked how most of their classmates would feel if they (the respondents) cheated on a test, the number answering "they wouldn't like it" dropped from 41 percent in 1976 to 15 percent in 1985. Probably more significant is the next statistic. The number of seniors thinking their classmates *would not care* jumped from 45 percent in 1976 to 80 percent in 1985.

Symbolic also of the sweeping change in values was youth's increased involvement in sexual activity. As a result in 1985 the United States had the highest teenage pregnancy rate of any industrialized nation. Between 1971 and 1982 the rate of increase in sexual activity for never-married girls between the ages of 15 and 19 averaged 59 percent. For girls aged 17, the increase during that eleven-year period was 100 percent (Hayes 1987).

Less obvious, perhaps, was the shift in the life purposes and goals of adolescents. Consider the life goal of "being very well off financially." The proportion of incoming college and university freshmen valuing wealth as an important goal increased to 70 percent by 1986, a 40 percent increase over what it registered ten years before. By contrast the life goal of "developing a meaningful philosophy of life" dropped precipitously. In 1970 it was the most valued goal (out of twenty) being endorsed by 83 percent of incoming college freshmen. By 1983–84 it had dropped to seventh on the list, being endorsed by only 45 percent (Astin 1985, p. 219). It is the considered judgment of Alexander Astin in his book, *Achieving Academic Excellence*, that "today's students are more materialistic and less altruistic, a reflection of the values of adult society" (p. 221).

Note how these value changes correlate with changes in the career plans of students. With endorsement of more materialistic and power-oriented values has come increased student interest in business, engineering, and computer science, as reflected in enrollment in college courses in these fields. Likewise the decline in altruism has been accompanied by decreased student interest in courses in education, social science, arts, humanities, nursing, social work, and ministry.

By 1986 the penalties that accompany a value system of self-gratification were on public display: tragic deaths through drugs, growing problems with alcoholism, more violence, child abuse, and incest in families, an increased rate of suicide, children having children, a life-threatening AIDS epidemic, and mounting divorce rates. Never before in the history of our country have we had such a marked upturn in self-destructive, life-denying behaviors as has typified the seventies and eighties.

One can expect that with this shift in motivation would come a much diminished cry of protest over social ills and a weakened offer to help. This less intense interest in righting society's wrongs is strikingly evident in the ten-year response of high-school seniors to a single item. The number willing to "spend much more time working with younger children," tumbled from 25 percent in 1976 to a lowly 3 percent in 1985. Likewise the number willing to give "somewhat more time" shrank from 32 percent to 18 percent. These two figures combined indicate a phenomenal decrease in youth's willingness to serve. The drop is from a total of 57 percent in 1976 who are ready to give "more time working with younger children" to 21 percent in 1985. Rarely does one see such dramatic changes in a trend analysis.

Significantly this shift in values toward self-fulfillment and self-actualization showed also in the changing commitment of parents to their children. Daniel Yankelovitch notes this in his book *New Rules*, based on his 1981 study of changing attitudes. "Today's parents expect to make fewer sacrifices for their children than in the past, but they also demand less from their offspring in the form of future obligations than their parents demanded" (pp. 103–104). He also notes that "a majority (66 percent) feel that 'parents should be free to live their own lives even if it means spending less time with their children'" (p. 104).

Changes among Church Youth

One can hope the erosion of youth's altruism might bypass church youth. But studies indicate otherwise. A ten-year comparison of 3,340 Lutheran high-school students in 1980 with 1,900 of their counterparts in 1970 provides a fair indication of shifts occurring among church youth in the seventies. There was a drop of 14 percentile points in their desire to serve others, a drop of 12 percentile points in involvement in helping activities, and a drop of 27 percentile points in charitable attitudes toward people commonly condemned. None of these lower scores can be attributed to chance factors (Strommen 1980, p. 4). Clearly for these church youth there was diminished motivation to help right the wrongs of society. The cry of protest or even of concern was being muted.

Similar results appear in Gupta's fifteen-year trend analysis of church youth. A dramatic drop in intensity appears in the concern of 1985 youth over national social issues. It is a drop of approximately twenty-two percentile points. This diminished concern for what is happening to people is accompanied by a slight decline in youth's desire to serve others in a meaningful way or press for needed changes. Significant too is the decline in these youth's attitude toward people commonly condemned by society, a decline that could not happen by chance more than once in twenty chances.[2] Though Gupta's 1985 sample may represent a more select group of church youth than did the 1970 sample, it still gives evidence that church youth are influenced by the massive value shift of the past fifteen years.

Intensifying the Cry

Many will agree that the muted cry of social concern needs to become full voice again. But reviving this cry would involve "altering the course of history" with respect to value trends for most youth. It would involve parents, congregational leaders, and youth pulling together purposefully. It would involve a deliberate effort to draw on resources unique to the Christian faith.

The conclusiveness of this statement is underscored in the 1986 report of the United States Department of Education, *What Works*. This summary of research presents as its very first finding the simple statement "Parents are their children's first and most influential teachers." It has been observed that the family is the original and most effective department of health, education, and welfare. If it fails to teach honesty, courage, the desire for excellence, and the values necessary for the welfare of humankind, it will be difficult for any other agency to make up for its failures. But the family needs help, a supporting cast. And this the congregation and its leaders must provide.

Adelson, author of *Inventing Adolescence* (1986), served as contributor to *A Nation at Risk*, the now-famous call for reform in the public schools. As a psychologist and authority on adolescence, he avers that in the arena of public schools the struggle is most intense between what he calls the values of traditionalism and those of modernity. The modernist ethos encourages sensual gratification rather than postponement of gratification; self-expression rather than self-restraint; deviant forms of family rather than family stability; ethical relativism rather than belief in certain moral universals. He believes that values present in today's public schools have been tipped in the direction of a modernist ethos. The task is to counter this drift by a renewed emphasis on teaching healthy concepts of right and wrong.

Significantly this is an emphasis parents welcome. In Search Institute's 1984 study of over ten thousand parents drawn randomly from eleven major denominations, parents' concern over the moral behavior of their children was impressive. When presented with a list of options regarding help they as parents might be given, the top choice was "To help my child develop healthy concepts of right and wrong." A total of 70 percent said they were "very" or "quite" interested in such help. (Strommen and Strommen 1985).

Delores Curran, in *Traits of a Healthy Family* (1983), speaks of being pleasantly surprised to see how highly 551 professionals rated the trait "teaches a sense of right and wrong." These professionals, who touch families through their work in education, church, health, and family counseling or volunteer organizations, ranked it number seven of a list of fifty-six possible characteristics of a healthy family. It is noteworthy that in a day when development of self tends to be given precedence, this group gives priority to the teaching of morality.

What are the implications of these findings for home and congregational activities? One implication is the need for accenting elements that strengthen youth's "immune system" and their ability to resist moral infections. In this regard research evidence is most encouraging. Our studies confirm that as youth's acceptance of moral beliefs goes up, their involvement in self-destructive activities goes down. As youth are helped to internalize moral beliefs, their immune system is strengthened, and they are able to say no to behaviors pressed on them by the mass media or their peer group. The implication is that families and churches need to discuss moral issues more explicitly. They need to do so quietly and rationally, showing how certain behaviors violate deep inner needs and disrupt relationships with others. This approach, known also as "induction," represents an effective way of helping youth internalize moral beliefs.

A second encouraging piece of evidence is found in characteristics of adolescents for whom a personal faith is central. We find these youth not only more likely to reject self-destructive activities but also more likely to be involved in serving and helping activities. Youth whose lives are rooted in faith, who live in awareness of God's promises, show an inner power that becomes evident in their behavior.

What are the implications of these findings? Two basic activities ought to characterize a congregation's youth and family ministries: teaching healthy concepts of right and wrong and leading youth into a conscious awareness of Christ as Lord and Savior.

There is a third implication that relates to service. In the past most congregations have tended to place their heaviest emphasis on preaching and teaching. A new accent is needed, namely, one showing that an important part of living a life of faith is reaching out in love to those who are overwhelmed by personal problems. Youth can be trained to become socially responsible for peers who are hurting. Friendship groups *can* become *intentionally* supportive to such youth. A good illustration of a program that does just this is Barbara Varnehorst's biblically based Peer Counseling Program (see note 6 for chapter 3). This is available nationally.

Immensely important in such teaching and awareness raising are parents who demonstrate a caring spirit themselves and make "doing the truth" a family experience. Together with their adolescent(s), they can address specific kinds of human need as an expression of their life of faith. Unfortunately not all parents associate meeting human need with their faith. The 1984 Young Adolescent study showed that parents are less likely than their children to believe that their Christian responsibility includes reaching out to people in acts of love and mercy (Strommen and Strommen 1985, p. 154).

This chapter, in identifying a major national trend toward greater self-enhancement and self-fulfillment, has not acknowledged the countertrends that have occurred for subpopulations of youth. While peer pressure and mass media push youth toward a more self-oriented life, there are less publicized but effective efforts to draw youth into meaningful service activities. A case in point surfaced in the 1985 study of 910 Catholic schools that serve almost a million high-school students. Its report noted that "service is one unique feature of Catholic schools": 93 percent of its schools offer service opportunities for their students and in nearly half of all schools off-campus service programs can be taken for credit (National Catholic Educational Association 1985). Clearly this effort has a shaping influence on youth's sense of social responsibility, a fact discussed in the following chapter.

Responding to the Cry

A fitting response to the smaller number whose cry is one of social concern is to establish forms of congregational life that express what is latent within a majority of adults. A congregation needs to say clearly, "We care," and to say it with a language of action.

More immediate steps are suggested by the kinds of help opportunities the young people prefer. From among descriptions of forty programs and activities that could be available in their churches, they chose their specific preferences and said, "I am very much interested and would go out of my way to participate."

Most attractive is belonging to a group where there is candor and caring among the members. Four out of five would go out of their way to attend meetings where people "felt free to say what they really think" and to experience acceptance among people "who really care about each other."

Three out of four express preference for a project that involves serving people in their community; they want training in being a friend to the lonely and rejected, insight into making changes in their schools, and growth in their concern and love for others. Truly there are youth in congregations who are willing to match rhetoric with action. Another interest relates to clarifying beliefs and values. Three out of four want to find meaning and purpose in life; they want exposure to people of other religious beliefs and chances to discuss their doubts and conflicts openly; they want to overcome their lack of self-confidence.

The eagerness of these youth to learn from adults is self-evident. Though oriented to change, they do not fit the newspaper stereotypes of youth who damn the establishment and listen only to their own age group.

Youth Reaching Youth

One of youth's concerns is their own age group. They worry about some of their contemporaries and wish they could reach out to them in a helping way. Given training, they can become an important resource for contacting lonely and alienated youth.

In 1970 Search Institute launched a three-year test of the relative effectiveness of three programs that train high-school youth to reach out to the friendless. The project, funded by the National Institute of Mental Health, involved 276 high-school juniors who met weekly for seventeen months of training and outreach. During this time they established friendships with 493 persons, some of whom were like the girl described by one of the junior volunteers.

She was teased unmercifully by so many, many kids—on the bus home, in school. She seemed so alone, and she didn't know how to keep kids from teasing her. She egged them on by her reactions; so many kids would come right out and be mean to her. I guess it looked like she needed to know there was someone who wouldn't always hound her.

A real and meaningful friendship, which lasted through most of the girl's senior year, was formed by the junior volunteer. Some indication of how this girl and the other 492 "reached" youth felt about the relationship appears in the following transcript of an interview.

Reached: I've known her (Project Youth volunteer) for about two years, but our friendship really started developing around the fall of this year. I came to her with a problem that I had gotten myself into trouble with, and she helped me. I had lost a few friends, and I was pretty much alone, by myself. And I didn't have my closest friend; we had sort of grown away from each other.

Interviewer: You have known her for approximately how many months?

Reached: Closely I've known her for about seven months. We're together in school every day, and we'll see each other off and on when we don't have classes.

She takes time to listen to me; she'll sit down if I have a problem, and she'll talk it out with me. Or if she notices that I'm doing something weird that she doesn't like in me and she doesn't think that it's good for me to do, she'll sit down and talk to me about it. She'll tell me; she'll just say what she feels. It's really nice to have somebody that will help you around. She'll listen to people; she'll listen to their problems. And she's an outgoing person; I really like her.

Interviewer: Any other points that you really like about her?

Reached: She's fun to be with. She and I have some common ideas and similar problems. We sort of came together. . . .

. . . I really like having a close friend, someone I can call up and say, "Hey, do you want to do something tonight?" Go over to her house or she'll come over to mine. Like my parents are going out for the weekend and she's coming over and staying with me; and go boating and sailing, all kinds of things. It's really good to have a close friend.

Observable changes in the behavior of the "reached" youth—some more than would be expected, a few well beyond expectation—were recorded.

These changes are listed in table 11 with an indication of *how many* were reported by sixty-three "reached" youth who were interviewed. Scores ranging from −2 to +2 indicate degree of positive or negative change. A score of +1 represents behavioral change that is better than would be expected. A score of 2 represents the best that could happen, as perceived by the reacher.

The purpose of this government-funded project was to assess the likelihood of training core youth in religious institutions to offer friendship to friendless youth. Not only was this purpose achieved, but the 274 reachers themselves benefited in observable ways: increased self-regard, greater willingness to participate in self-disclosure with persons not too distant from them, fewer fears about being accepted by others, and increased self-confidence. Socially concerned youth profit from training opportunities and prove effective in reaching lonely peers.

Table 11
Changes in the Behavior of "Reached" Youth

No. of Reached Youth	Dimension of Growth	Degree of Change
3	Consideration for others	+ 1.67
7	Ability to establish and carry out goals regarding education	+ 1.29
4	Reduction in drug use	+ 1.25
16	Ability to confide in others	+ .94
7	Ability to cope with school responsibilities	+ .71
6	Ability to communicate with the opposite sex	+ .71
16	Sense of worth and confidence	+ .69
3	Church participation and strengthening of faith	+ .67
20	Ability to make and keep friends	+ .65
13	Ability to communicate with parents	+ .42
6	Trusting and accepting of others	+ .42
7	Ability to face problems, accept criticism, and make decisions	+ .36

5. Cry of the Prejudiced

We want God's commandments to be followed, not preached out both sides of mouths.

Sabine

Psychologist James Dittes, writing about prejudice and religion in *Research on Religious Development* (1971), makes this important point. The Scriptures cite two types of "believers"—those for whom religion is a thoughtful commitment affecting the total person and those for whom religion is a formal and externalized response. Old Testament prophets distinguished between solemn assemblies that were a mockery and a righteousness that is like an overflowing stream, between burnt offerings that are a duty and a knowledge of God that is coupled with a steadfast love.

Christ underscored the distinction between public, overt, institutionalized, self-serving religion and an inner response of contrition, trust, commitment, and dedication. He made uncompromising attacks on the pious Pharisees, saying, "They do all their deeds to be seen by men." Addressing the Pharisees, he said, "You tithe . . . but neglect the weightier matters of . . . mercy. . . . You are sons of those who murdered the prophets" (Mt. 23:23–31 RSV). He clearly denounced people who use religion for personal gain, who are willing to destroy whoever threatens them or their establishment.

Since the days of Christ and the prophets people have made similar observations about the religion of man. Kierkegaard distinguished between "official Christianity" and the "radical Christian." Barth and others made distinctions between Christianity and religion. Let us illustrate in terms of a fictional young person.

One thing you can say for Church—when his youth group is meeting, he is usually there. He prides himself on seldom missing a meeting, as though he has earned something to which more casual members of the group are not entitled.

Chuck is selfish about his group. His slowness to accept new members sometimes irritates others, and several members were embarrassed by his behavior when one member brought a foreign exchange student from Africa to a meeting. It takes new people a long time to gain Chuck's respect and confidence.

He tends not be very accepting of people who haven't made up their minds about discussion issues or who disagree with him. His "convictions" are stereotyped prejudgments that he accepts, in closed-mind fashion, and champions. He knows where he stands on legalization of marijuana, abortion, current political issues, questions of dating behavior, and the rehabilitation of those who break the law. Once he has expressed his opinion, no matter what else turns up during the discussion, Chuck rarely changes his mind.

Worship appears to be important to him, but he is less enthusiastic about participating in an improvised worship service during a contemporary celebration of worship on a weekend retreat. It does not seem to him that he has really gone to church.

Though fairly well accepted by most of his group, he is roundly opposed when he sounds off on social issues.

Social scientists have found prejudice in people who adhere to social forms of religion and not in those who "take religion seriously in a more internalized sense." Adorno and others (1950) noted that prejudiced people "seem to make use of religious ideas in order to gain some immediate practical advantage or aid in the manipulation of people."

Gordon Allport, noting this utilitarianism, distinguished between "intrinsic" and "extrinsic" religious persons. Extrinsically religious persons use their religion, and the intrinsically religious live theirs, says Allport. The extrinsic personality institutionalizes religion; the intrinsic person wants an "interiorized" faith.

This distinction provides understanding of youth like Chuck—the sometimes pious but prejudiced. Their profiles express an attitude that unfortunately appears within the Christian church at large. It is the cry of racists and bigots who pride themselves on being self-made people. "Don't disturb our little world," they say. "Don't let outsiders in." It is the cry of people whose religion is self-effort and whose goal is achieving a place in the sun, even at the price of stepping on others. Although it is more common among people advanced in years, our findings indicate that this outlook is alive and active among youth as well.

Allen and Spilka, building on the early studies already mentioned, offer a distinction between "committed religious" and "consensual religious." Briefly the criteria groups were these.[1]

The "committed religious" conceptualize their faith in relational expressions; they speak of their faith with clarity, make distinctions that show an awareness of complex issues, are thoughtful about their beliefs, open to new insights, and show that their faith is a personal concern and of central importance. They seek to make it relevant to daily activities.

The "consensual religious" conceptualize their faith in specific dos and don'ts, they speak of it in vague and conventional statements, they oversimplify the issues, resist differing ideas and insist always that theirs are the right beliefs. The consensual rarely apply their faith in daily activities and behavior. (Allen and Spilka 1967, p. 14)

Allen and Spilka found that two out of three "consensual" respondents were prejudiced, but no more than one out of ten of the "committed" were.

These two orientations are parallel to the law orientation and gospel orientation of *A Study of Generations*. In this chapter we will adopt the consensual-committed distinction. It should be understood that some youth fall between the two orientations by combining both emphases to a relatively equal degree. And some espouse and manifest *neither* to any great degree.

Do-It-Yourself Religion

More than youth of the other four groups, the consensual religionist holds to a generalized religion that stresses man's effort for achieving the favor of God. Their quite consistent theological stance is noteworthy because consistency of response to doctrinal items is not a characteristic of church youth generally. Even committed youth who embrace the Christian faith with enthusiasm and participate actively in their congregations have not learned to make the theological distinction.

The following data shows how many youth consistently accept or reject items associated with achieving God's favor.

83%—"The way to be accepted by God is to try sincerely to live a good life" (yes or not sure).

75%—The above statement *and* "God is satisfied if a person lives the best life he can" (yes or not sure).

49%—The two above statements *and* "If I say I believe in God and do right I will get to heaven" (yes or not sure).

42%—The three above statements *and* "I believe a person at birth is neither good nor bad" (yes or not sure).

32%—All of the above statements with an exclusive yes to the first item.

Figure 5. Characteristics of Prejudiced Youth

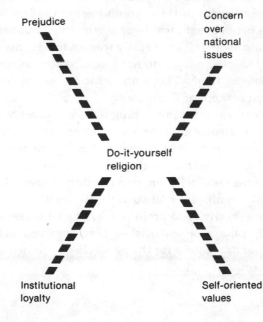

Prejudice

Concern over national issues

Do-it-yourself religion

Institutional loyalty

Self-oriented values

If church youth in general have not formulated a consistent theology, how do youth labeled consensual differ in what they believe? A sample was drawn of 538 youth who most resemble the characteristics given in figure 5. (They score in the lower quarter on biblical concepts, the lower half on human relations, and the upper half on adult caring.) A profile emerges when we compare these 538 youth with the other 6,512.

Consensual youth exhibit greater consistency in affirming that salvation is gained by earning God's pleasure. Almost unanimously they agree that "to try sincerely to live a good life" is the way to be accepted by God. It matters little to them what one believes as long as he is sincere and lives the best life he can. The gospel for these youth is essentially composed of God's rules for right living. Whoever follows God's rule book—the Bible—and plays the game right will make it. Everyone can win if he or she chooses to because people are born neither good nor bad. Outside intervention does not appear to be an essential ingredient in man's relationship to God. Christianity is viewed simplistically as something man does (see table 12).

The you-can-do-it-if-you-try conviction described here seems to color the attitudes of these youth toward the less fortunate. Two-thirds believe that most people who live in poverty could do something about it if they really wanted to. Seventy-two percent agree that poor people do not take advantage of opportunities available to them. The work ethic is tied up with their achievement concept of Christianity.

The dominant and distinguishing feature of consensual youth appears to be greater consistency in affirming a religion that stresses achievement, right living, and doing the best one can. They are quite united in accepting what is variously called a folk religion, a consensus religion, or a religion in general.

It is highly significant that such youth should also be distinguished by a proclivity to prejudice. Though a cause-and-effect relationship cannot be established between these beliefs and prejudice, our data allows for the possibility by showing that the two are linked.

Table 12
How Consensual Youth Perceive Christianity

Item			No	Yes	?
			Percentage Response		
The way to be accepted by God is to try sincerely to live a good life	Consensual	Youth	0	96	4
	Other Church	Youth	17	60	18
Being tolerant means that one accepts all religions— including Christianity—as equally important before God	Consensual	Youth	0	59	40
	Other Church	Youth	18	48	31
God is satisfied if a person lives the best life he can	Consensual	Youth	0	94	6
	Other Church	Youth	15	67	16
I believe a person at birth is neither good nor bad	Consensual	Youth	0	75	25
	Other Church	Youth	17	63	17
Salvation depends upon being sincere in whatever you believe	Consensual	Youth	0	73	26
	Other Church	Youth	16	54	27
The main emphasis of the Gospel is on God's rules for right living	Consensual	Youth	0	77	23
	Other Church	Youth	19	51	27
Although there are many religions in the world, most of them lead to the same God	Consensual	Youth	0	88	12
	Other Church	Youth	16	63	19
If I say I believe in God and do right, I will get to heaven	Consensual	Youth	0	53	45
	Other Church	Youth	35	29	31

Another feature of consensual church youth is their expression of religious earnestness. Seventy-three percent say they have a sense of being saved in Christ, as opposed to 52 percent of other church youth; as "saved" youth they declare a fervency about their faith. They express great interest in experiencing a closer relationship to God, finding meaning and purpose in life, and finding God's will for them. They say they would go out of their way to participate in activities that would help them achieve these objectives.

In spite of an avowed religiousness that is well above average, their practices of personal piety (incidence of Bible reading, private prayer, church attendance, or percentage giving) do not differ from church youth generally. Nor do they excel in sharing their faith or serving others. Their greater religiousness seems to be primarily verbal; though they use the pious words of a special relationship to the Christian faith, they lack visible evidence of a changed relationship.

Characteristics of Prejudice

If verbal assent to a prejudiced statement is a valid indication of prejudice, then we can say something about the extent to which it is found among church youth.

Prejudice is a respecter of age, increasing its corrosive effects to some degree as the years advance. During their youthful years people are most open to those different from themselves and least given to passing judgment on others[2]. For that reason we can expect a fairly low percentage of prejudiced church youth.

Two out of ten church youth express prejudiced attitudes (using the twenty items that assess a generalized prejudice), and three out of ten are not sure whether to agree or disagree with statements that reflect prejudice. Some say, "I really haven't thought much about it"; others who use the question-mark response are inclined to believe the prejudgment, saying, "There may be some truth in it; where there's smoke there's usually fire." On the average, one out of two church youth resolutely reject statements that are prejudiced, punitive in attitude, or inhumane.

Predictors of Prejudice

A willingness to discriminate on the basis of race or color is more likely to be found among the 538 consensual youth than among all other church youth. More of them will either agree with an obvious statement of bias or say they are not sure about their opinion. (We have found that question-mark answers to racial items are more likely to indicate prejudice rather than a positive attitude.)

Anti-Semitism finds fertile soil among the consensual religionists. Fewer reject obviously stereotyped prejudgments of Jews, and many more than usual hide in the woods of a question-mark response. For instance, if someone says that Jews are more likely to cheat in business, less than one-fifth of the consensual youth will agree, but two-thirds of them will declare they are not sure. Only a few agree to the comment, "Jews are not bound by Christian ethics, therefore they do things to get ahead that Christians would never do," but more than two-thirds declare their uncertainty.

There is less ambiguity in how they feel about blacks. A majority either agree or say they are "not sure" that blacks and whites should not intermingle socially. Whenever the "agree" responses are added to the "not sure" answers on items indicating racial prejudice, there is always a majority among this consensual group.

In *A Study of Generations,* also, a strong association consistently shows up between prejudice (toward Jews, blacks, or poor people) and a religion of standards and meritorious living.[3]

We do find bigotry and prejudice within Lutheranism, as our understanding of man, even Christian man, would suggest; however, we fail to find that prejudice is related to the belief system most central to Lutherans, namely, the Heart of Lutheran Piety. (Factor 1.)

Rather we find prejudice strongly connected with generalized rigidity of personality, and to a lesser extent with misbeliefs and heresies, many of which are not unique to Christianity. Church law-oriented persons, threatened by change, are prone to attitudes of prejudice; prejudiced persons are apt to cling to a law orientation. (Strommen et al. 1972, p. 212)

The youth most susceptible to prejudging others are identified by certain of the thirty-nine characteristics that we tested. First and foremost is an unthinking approach to life. The strongest indicator of prejudice is the frank admission "I seldom think about why I believe and act as I do." Apparently education that stimulates young people to think, probe, weigh facts, and face issues is a necessary antidote to the poison of prejudice.

Ranking next is the simple acknowledgment "My opinions on race relations are more conservative than one or both of my parents." What causes this is not known. Because it is usual for young people to be more liberal in their attitudes than are their parents, the opposite tendency is especially noteworthy.

The 14 percent of our ecumenical sample who embody the two criteria given above show by low human relations scores that they qualify as fledgling bigots. They tend to place their highest value on money (plenty of money for things I want); few are bothered when they hear and see minorities abused; and a disproportionate number have low grades or have dropped out of school altogether.

Reversing the coin, we find that the *least* prejudiced youth think through what they believe and do, tend to draw excellent or above-average grades, and are strongly oriented to change. For them money tends to rank low in value, and transcendental (meaning sought through relationship with others and God) values are high; most are involved in social action, along with members of their families. The least prejudiced are far more likely to know a personal, caring God but at the same time are critical of adult members for not seeming to "care."

Unquestioning Institutional Loyalty

Consensual youth make compliant church members. They are less likely to question what they are taught, to doubt the existence of God, or to puzzle over the divinity of Christ. They take a rosy view of the way things are. More are happy with their church (76 percent versus 53 percent of other church youth) and say they are inspired by the Sunday morning services. Fewer are critical of adult members (e.g., their stand on social issues), and fewer are ready to fault the adults' concern over or response to human need.

It is the impression of most consensual youth that adult members care a lot for each other. Seventy-three percent (versus 48 percent of other church youth) believe there is an openness to diversity and will cite efforts to bring together youth and adults for an interchange of viewpoints. Three out of four insist that people who are quite different (richer, poorer, another race, dress, hair) would be welcome in their church. They feel the same about how their friends would be received: "My church is interested in my age group."

The unrealistic evaluations of many seem evident in their answer to the item "Most adults in my congregation would be able to tell you what the purpose of our church is." A total of 62 percent of the consensual youth say yes. Thirty-six percent of all other church youth make a similar evaluation and only 19 percent of one denomination's clergy make a similar evaluation. But maybe the evaluation is an accurate one from their point of view and their concept of purpose. If attending and supporting a church is a good deed, then many adult members may be quite clear as to why they are active—it is to fulfill an obligation and gain merit with God.

Loyalty to the church's youth group is abundantly in evidence for the religious achievers. A high percentage are delighted with their group, sense its progress, enjoy being with the members, and feel a real spirit of togetherness. In only one critique do they agree with church youth in general—few report an openness and freedom to share in depth some of the troubling issues of their lives. Though there is camaraderie and an esprit de corps, it is an arm's-length fellowship.

The families of consensual youth are as close-knit and religious as other church families. No more, no less. More of them, however, do admit to some racial bias in their homes. They are not free to invite persons of other races into their homes, and about half believe (or are not sure) that their families would support neighborhood efforts to keep out people of other races.

Self-Oriented Values

The balance on values tips in the direction of self-development. Consensual youth favor goals related to their interests rather than those that seek meaning through relationships with other persons (e.g., service, ethical life, love) and with the divine (e.g., eternal life, religion, salvation). This characteristic, however, is a weak one and cannot be stressed. It is a tendency reflected in the data and no more. Hints of this value preference appear especially for the most prejudiced youth. They tend to place high value on the acquisition of money (for things I want) and to be unperturbed when minority people are abused or treated maliciously.

Concern over National Issues

Another characteristic about which little can be said is the greater distress of consensual youth over national issues. This characteristic too is a weak one, and no more can be said than to identify it as a tendency. It bears mentioning, however, because it calls to mind the times when white adults have massed to protest when blacks have moved into their communities.

Components of Prejudice

From the evidence supplied by a partially formed profile we can draw the following conclusions:

About one in seven church youth embody the prejudice that haunts the Christian church. They differ from other church youth in their consistent belief that acceptance with God is earned by meritorious living. They are less reflective and thoughtful and hence prone to think in stereotypes and make prejudgments. They rank lower than other church youth in academic achievement and are somewhat more self-seeking in their values. (One wonders about the degree to which intelligence accounts for these variables.)

The striking evidence that consensual youth are more likely to speak of "being saved" suggests that these youth want to talk a good game, even though they don't play an unusually good one. They believe that the successful Christian life consists of living by certain rules, coming up to certain standards; their interest in being successful at whatever they try—including the "Christian life" game—causes them to pad their scores a little. To give a testimony, to conform to certain practices, is for some a way to gain status. What they call a conversion—even though highly emotional—may be little more than a change of institutional allegiance. It lacks the change in orientation and values that accompanies a profound conversion.

Has the Cry Changed?

For a while, prejudice in the United States was declining. Seymour Lipsit, in his review of studies since 1964, contends that bigotry has declined steadily since World War II and positive attitudes toward minorities have increased (Lipsit 1987, p. 5). A survey by the National Opinion Research Center in 1963 showed that 55 percent of Americans agreed with the statement "White people have a right to keep (Negroes/blacks) out of their neighborhoods if they want to, and (Negroes/blacks) should respect that right." By 1985, the number of Americans agreeing to that statement had declined to 26 percent, a drop of 29 percent. A similar shift in attitudes can be documented with respect to Jews. A 1981 survey by Yankelovitch, employing the fifteen-item measure of negative beliefs about Jews used in a 1964 survey by the Anti-Defamation League, showed a drop from 33 to 24 percent of those holding negative feelings about Jews. Such findings led Yehuda Bauer, head of the International Center for the Study of Anti-Semitism to observe that "in the past few decades the level of popular anti-Semitism in Western countries has been waning" (Lipsit 1987, p. 4). In 1987, estimates regarding the number of Americans holding prejudiced views toward minorities revolved around one in four.

Though denounced, bigotry still remains a formidable enemy. For example, Asian Americans, once objects of more bitterness and intolerance than blacks, are now accepted and admired as a model minority. But homegrown hatred by people jealous of this success has been escalating in a cycle of anti-Asian incidents. Friction between Asian immigrants and blacks is a big issue in a number of American inner cities today (Zinsmeister 1987, p. 9). Likewise, whites threatened by the work ethic of

Asians and their economic success have been guilty of gross examples of bigotry and cruelty.

Has this cry changed for youth? The few measures of prejudice that span a period of time indicate that concern over race relations has diminished between the years 1976 and 1985 and then showed a distinct rise in 1988. Among high school seniors a significant increase of 11% occurred of those who worry "some" or "often" about race relations (Table 13).

This rise in concern over race relations anticipates the racial violence which has characterized 1991 and 1992 in various cities of the country. In Brooklyn, New York, conflict between Hasidic Jews and African-American youth and adults exploded into four nights of rioting. In Washington, D.C. anger between Hispanics and the mainly black police department resulted in two nights of rioting. In Los Angeles, the court's exoneration of police involved in the beating of a black motorist, triggered nights of burning and looting that spread to major cities around the country.

This breakdown in race relations was not uniquely American. The dismantling of the old order in East and West Europe surfaced ethnic tensions that had been repressed for decades. In every country sampled in East Europe, at least 40% felt hostile to the main national minority—Poles in Germany, Gypsies in Poland, Jews in Hungary, etc. (Kushnick, 1992). The year 1992 saw tragic scenes of bloody wars between ethnic groups. Youth, heavily influenced by adult attitudes and behaviors, shared in these battles. These reports of ethnic violence in the nineties stand in sharp contrast to attitudes in the eighties. An illustration of this is found in the responses of 7,551 students in the 1984 Catholic study of parochial schools serving low-income students. The random sample of ninth and twelfth grade students in 106 low-income-serving schools included 1,675 blacks, 1,105 Hispanics, 186 Asians, 163 native Americans, and 4,150 whites. When faced with the item "Discrimination against minorities is no longer a problem in our country," 78 percent of the blacks, 79 percent of the Hispanics, and 73 percent of the white students agreed. When asked, "How right or wrong is it for people in the neighborhood to be trying to keep a minority family from moving in?"

Table 13
**Thirteen-Year Comparison of Seniors'
Attitudes toward Race Relations**

Item	1976	1988
How often do you worry about race relations?		
Never	12%	18%
Seldom	34	28
Some	34	32
Often	21	22
How much have you gotten to know people of other races in church?		
Not at all	44%	35%
A little	17	18
Some	12	14
A lot	7	10
Does not apply	20%	23%

again the response was high. Those answering "always wrong" or "usually wrong" totaled 89 percent for blacks, 91 percent for Hispanics, and 84 percent for whites.

In spite of these responses, the lurking presence of prejudice can still be discerned, as in the responses of these students to the following items:

Minorities are getting too demanding in their push for equal rights.

Over the past few years minorities have gotten more economically than they deserve.

Over the past few years the government and news media have shown more respect to minorities than they have deserved.

One in four of the white students in these Catholic parochial schools agreed with the above statements in contrast to one in seven of the Hispanics and one in ten of the blacks.

A ten-year comparison (1970–80) of Lutheran youth however, showed a reverse trend. Using the highly reliable measure of human relations, we found a marked decline in sensitivity and compassion toward persons often criticized or judged harshly.

This decline was even greater for the 954 non-Lutheran students attending the parochial schools. It was the equivalent of a drop from fifty to twenty-two percentile points. Paralleling this drop in charitable attitudes was a sharp drop in students' concern over national issues such as injustice, poverty, nuclear warfare, and violence. This too plummeted from fifty percentile points to thirty-one.

Significant evidence such as the above suggested that fewer church youth in 1980 were accepting of people commonly condemned by society than typified church youth in 1970.

Changes among Church Youth

Has the cry of prejudice changed for church youth? The most conclusive answer is found in Gupta's fifteen-year trend analysis. For church youth in 1985, there is a slight decline over 1970 in youth's measure of human relations—that is, fewer church youth in 1985 expressed charitable attitudes toward minorities and people commonly judged harshly. The decline, much less than what was reported by Lutheran youth in 1980, still cannot be attributed to chance factors five times in a hundred (see footnote 2 of Chapter 4). Possibly more indicative of a shift in attitude is the decline in youth's concern over what is happening to hurting, maligned, unjustly treated people in our country. The drop in concern over such national issues (noted in the previous chapter) is striking. It represents a drop of at least twenty percentile points.

Has the cry changed? Worldwise it has. And to a degree it has changed for some church youth. Our measures show an increase in prejudice and less concern over the welfare of others. Though a significant minority of church youth, they represent only about 15 percent of church youth.

The Educational Process

The Christian church has a heritage of values, beliefs, way of life, and practices that center in the person of Christ. One task of parents and congregations, is to transmit this inheritance and make the accumulated riches and insights of the Christian church available to young people. Passing on a faith, however, has its dangers. It can stress an orientation that has negative effects. It can require that beliefs be accepted unquestioningly, insist on ways of behaving, and draw attention away from God's intervention in the lives of people and instead emphasize the dos and don'ts.

Direction

Bel Kaufman's book *Up the Down Staircase* (1972) concerns a teacher in a New York high school who repeatedly makes the mistake of going up a staircase intended for downward traffic. The metaphor aptly describes the youth of this chapter; they are intent on going *up* a staircase of Christianity that God designed for *down* traffic. Gerhard Forde, in *Where God Meets Man* (1972), calls this attempt to struggle upward toward perfection "staircase," or "ladder," theology. It contrasts with a faith that God comes down the staircase and gives life to people wherever they are.

Historically Christianity has emphasized that God became incarnate in Jesus Christ and that he lived and died on earth to bring life to man. The message of the Christian church is essentially a "down staircase" story that emphasizes what God has done, is doing, and will do.

The issue in consensual youth's answers to belief items is essentially one of direction. It is not that they gave answers differing from what their church teaches but that they attribute divine importance to their actions. This distinction is serious because prejudice is linked with an "up staircase" theology.

Openness

In the New Testament the Greek word for *doubt* is used in two different ways. Most frequently it is translated as "to discern, to discriminate, to make distinctions, to examine, to scrutinize." In other words, doubt is a state of open-mindedness in which one sees for himself or herself and becomes personally convinced.

This aspect of doubt is to be encouraged. Youth need a Christianity that is not a borrowed tradition but a new life lived with conviction. The task is to provide freedom for questioning and searching while expressing and demonstrating Christian commitment.

The positive value of open-mindedness must not, however, conceal the reality of the second meaning of doubt, that of being of two minds, capable of the unwillingness to give oneself to God. Some doubts are rooted not in a need for answers but in a need for doubts. They are traceable not to seeking the truth but to an obstinacy of the mind, unwillingness to accept, and even hatred of the truth. It is closed-mindedness. In this sense doubt is a sinful effort to deny God and the implications of commitment.

A good way to dissolve doubt is to hear and accept the story of who God is and therefore who we are. Faith comes by hearing this word of God. This faith in turn leads to an acknowledgment of sinfulness and a surrender to his will; it leads us to accept the God who comes "down the staircase" to man.

Openness to truth and openness to God are lacking in many youth. They do not want their stereotypes disturbed. This is precisely what the educational process must do; it must force one to question his or her prejudgments and boilerplate answers to life. An educational process in home and church should teach youth to speak the language *about* faith and the language *of* faith.[4]

The language *about* faith (statements of doctrine)
   —involves generalizations about Christian truth
   —involves religious knowledge
   —expresses an intellectual perception
   —reflects a person seeking clarity of thought
   —deals with doubt directed at truths
The language *of* faith (statements that speak of what God has done and is doing)
   —involves statements about a living God

—involves words of love and relationship quite unrelated
to knowledge
—expresses one's earnestness
—reflects a person committed to the person of Jesus Christ
—deals with self-doubt

I have accented the educational process of passing on truths
and truth incarnate because the Old and New Testaments stress
this responsibility. Furthermore our research shows that persistent efforts at Christian education do open minds and hearts. It
also shows that the human equation—the teacher or parent—is
a vital one. When teachers are open to God and to other people,
when they reflect a spirit of freedom and conviction, their pu-
pils are drawn toward their teachers' faith. But the parent or
teacher who is occupied with no-no's either repels the young
person by his or her distortion of Christianity or gains a convert
for the crowd going up the down staircase.

The close link between the beliefs of youth and parents is
strikingly illustrated in the study described below. Closed-mindedness in adult parents is associated with closed-mindedness
or rebellion in their children. Faith and an openness in spirit
among parents is associated with a similar attitude in their
youth.

Parental Influence

The case has been made, through numerous research studies,
that the most significant agent in the process of religious education is the family. When a home is characterized by congeniality
children are most likely to admire their parents and want to be
like them. When the orientation of the family is religious the
impact of outside factors (e.g., parochial school education) may
be minimized except in reinforcing values the home has already
established.

Using data from a 1968 national survey, we tested the thesis
that congenial home atmosphere, coupled with parental religiousness, is likely to produce youth who share the faith of their

parents. To a national study of one thousand randomly selected high-school youth (Evangelical Covenant) we added an interesting feature. A parent of each youth was asked to participate in the study in this way. As the child answered two hundred survey items assessing his or her concerns, the parents in another room responded to the same items as *they thought their child was answering them* (neither was aware of what was being asked of the other). It is assumed that if a parent and child answer similarly, this indicates a degree of closeness and understanding between the parent and youth. If the parent's answers bear no resemblance to the youth's self-report, the assumption is they are strangers to each other.

To test the similarity between the parent's and child's answers, we computed their correlation. If, for instance, a father's answers parallel those of his child, the correlation is unity, or 1. If there is no congruence between the two sets of answers, there is no correlation, or zero.

We found that one mother anticipated her child's answers so perfectly that the correlation was almost unity, or 1. It was .99. Some were so lacking in perception that the correlation coefficient went below zero to a negative correlation. Parents' perceptions were the opposite of what the young person reported about himself or herself.

Correlations for the 960 parents in the study ranged from −.16 to +.99. This information alone is useful because it shows why the static concept of a generation gap is a poor one. The social distance between parents and youth ranges from near to far. Some parents are unusually close to their children and show their perceptiveness in correlations above .60. Others err in the accuracy of their perception, having no idea how their child thinks or feels.

Findings in the study of parent–child relationships

Is accurate perception or empathy important? We chose 150 parents whose scores correlated best with their child's and 150 parents whose scores showed no correlation. The youth least congruent with their parents contrasted sharply with those most congruent on dimensions associated with self-esteem and religious commitment. They contrasted in their beliefs, religious earnestness, personal practices or moral behavior, and degree of concern.

The "least understood" youth were less believing and less religiously earnest; they were more given to questionable practices and more troubled over personal feelings. The "most understood youth" tended to express a personal faith and a religious commitment. They also showed greater emotional stability and less inclination toward questionable or unethical practices.

What accounts for this difference? Because causation is involved, an answer cannot be given. Correlational studies can only prove the absence of causation—they cannot establish *what* causes *what*.

The data, however, support the thesis of a study that isolated two important variables in communicating a religious faith, each essential to the other. One is a congenial relationship between parents and youth, and the other is religious commitment in the parent.

Does congeniality characterize the relationship of high-correlating parents with their children? Here is how we answered that question. When each parent and child finished the survey, they were asked to fill out a sentence-completion questionnaire.

For the parent: "My relationship with my teenager (the one here) is ———."

For the child: "My relationship to my parent (the one involved in this study) is ———."

The child of one noncorrelating parent wrote: "My mother is a bitch, a snob, and a nosy Holy Roller. I despise her." The parent of that child showed her lack of perceptiveness by answering that her relationship with her teenager was " . . . a good one—we are close, and I feel she often confides in me and desires to please. We are pals."

By way of contrast note what the child of the most highly correlating parent wrote:

I love my parents very much! Both of them. I feel they are the perfect parents. As far as my relationship is concerned, I suppose I am very close to both of them. My age (15) has probably something to do with it. The fact that I am always depending on them for everything is probably the reason I am so close to them. After I graduate from high school and college, I *know* I will feel the same way as I do now! I have known and seen worse parents, but I can't say I've seen any better. I love my parents very much, and I have no problems they can't solve.

The parent of the child quoted above was far more tentative about his relationship. The father described his relationship with his teenager as " . . . somewhat close."

These quotes, though selected, do illustrate the high association we found between a congenial relationship and the accuracy of parental empathy or perception. It would be accurate to say that a high correlation between parent and youth scores indicates an understanding parent and an open and sharing child. This becomes especially apparent in the process to be described.

We divided the parents into five groups according to the degree their survey answers correlated with their child's.

Group 1—correlations below zero (negative)
Group 2—correlations .00 to .29
Group 3—correlations .30 to .39
Group 4—correlations .40 to .49
Group 5—correlations .50 and above

Having read what the children of each group wrote about their relationship with their parents, we rated the quality as good, fair, or bad. A congenial relationship was considered a good one. In like fashion the sentence completions by parents in each group were read and rated as more or less congruent (accurate) with what the child said.

The results were fascinating. As shown in table 14 the percentage of young people whose comments reflected a good parental relationship increased steadily as the correlation approached .50 or above. They began with 42 percent and increased to 100 percent. Likewise the percentage of parents

Table 14
Comparison of Family Relationships

Item	Below 0 N=21	0-.19 N=20	.3-.39 N=21	.4-.49 N=20	.50+ N=18
	Correlation Range				
YOUTH					
My relationship to my parent is					
Good	42%	50%	79%	75%	100%
Fair	38	29	5	10	0
Bad	21	21	16	15	0
PARENT					
My relationship with my teenager is					
Congruent answer	36%	50%	84%	90%	100%
Noncongruent answer	64	50	16	10	0

whose answers were congruent with their child's began at 36 percent and increased to 100 percent for those with correlations of .50 or above.

In general the higher the correlation, the more likely it is that a parent resonates with son or daughter, that the youth reports a congenial or close relationship with his or her parent.

One cannot assume, of course, that the accurate perception of a parent causes a cordial relationship. It can work either way. For instance, the parents whose lines of communication are open, who accord psychological freedom for their children to express themselves, and who have learned to listen for unspoken feelings as well as to what their child actually says are best able to answer a survey as they think their children are answering the items. A parent's close relationship to a child makes it possible to anticipate quite accurately the child's thoughts, attitudes, and feelings.

It is well to note that many youth (42 percent) speak of a close relationship even though their parents indicate no understanding of how they feel. This suggests that there are factors other than accuracy of perception that bind youth and parents together in a good relationship. Parent and child may be close even though one does not understand the other.

To what degree might the nature of the religious faith of parents make a difference? To answer this question we examined the self-reports of parents regarding what they themselves actually believed, valued, and did. We noted especially the profiles and descriptive data of the 150 high-correlating and the 150 low-correlating parents. Parents in the two groups were very much alike in most areas under comparison (e.g., socioeconomic level, educational background, religious involvement, and so on). Where they differed markedly was in their perception of the Christian faith. Low-correlating parents tended to view Christianity as a religion of works—something one did. The high-correlating parents tended to view Christianity as a religion of grace—something one accepts as a gift.

These two types of religionists—we will call them the law-oriented (preoccupied with standards and demands) and gospel-oriented (preoccupied with promise and possibilities)—are similar to the two types of adult church members identified in *A Study of Generations*, who contrast both in their perception of Christianity and in their view of people. Law-oriented parents tend to be authoritarian and overcontrolling in their approach to family life.

The differences in religious faith of the high- and low-correlating parents support the conclusion that a committed, intrinsic Christian faith is best communicated by adults who are not only accurate in their empathic relationships but also gospel oriented in their faith. In other words, parental openness and perceptiveness with respect to a religious faith, plus an openness and perceptiveness with respect to one's children, are highly associated with a similar religious faith in those children.

Coping with a Changing Society

The cry of prejudice in the setting of a Christian congregation is increasingly unwelcome in today's changing world. Prejudice on the basis of race, color, economic level, health, age, sex, or ability contradicts the gospel, in which "there is neither Jew nor Greek, there is neither slave nor free, there is neither male nor female; for you are all one in Christ Jesus" (Gal. 3:28, RSV). Note why this issue is growing in importance in our society.

Immigration patterns and differential fertility rates are significantly changing our nation's social composition. Taking immigration as an example, consider that in 1984 two-thirds of all immigrants in the world entered the United States. These people tended to be from the middle class of their respective countries; they were well educated and eager to see their children achieve. Almost one-third of these world immigrants came to California.

Let us look at the statistics on fertility rates. For white American women the rate is 1.7 percent. For black women it is 2.4 percent, and for Mexican-American women it is 2.9 percent, the same rate as it was for white women during the so-called baby boom. In the United States the average Hispanic American is only twenty-three years old. This means that white Americans are moving out of their childbearing years just as black and Hispanic Americans are entering them (Hodgkinson 1986). It is predicted that by the year 2000 one out of three Americans will be nonwhite. Increasingly minorities will be a part of our nation's suburbs as well as its inner cities. They will be people contributing to our middle class and our underclass. A growing number of American youth will be poor, from broken homes, and psychologically scarred. They will contribute an increasing number to a population that will largely be supported by the government (Hodgkinson 1984, p. 14). The cry of prejudice threatens to increase in stridency and advocacy in response to such dramatic change.

What are the implications? The time seems right to launch a long-range program of learning how to welcome and serve increasingly diverse members in our congregations. For years the members of most mainline denominations have been primarily white. Intrinsic to the message of the gospel is the spirit of welcome to the stranger, the poor, and people of other races. Providing services to a wider community of people helps to counter the ever-present danger of a self-centered piety.

Thoughtful people draw attention to the institutionalized nature of prejudice. They insist that "the way to break down an unreasonable custom is to contradict it in practice." Or as an ardent opponent of prejudice, Thomas Pettigrew, would insist, "to change the attitude, you have to change the behavior" (Kimmel 1986, p. 51). Interestingly one way Christ defined love was in terms of welcoming the stranger, feeding the hungry, clothing the naked, and visiting those in prison.

Postscript

This chapter has drawn attention to the tendency to live by stereotypes and prejudgments. Some youth are especially afflicted with this disease of utilitarianism, a self-centered preoccupation with advancement, security, and one's own little world. Whatever disturbs this insecure world meets the irrational response of a fearful person.

A minority of young people succumb to the disease. Fortunately the challenge of new ideas and the stimulus of parents and teachers keep the minds of the majority alive and willing to struggle with prejudice.

A ministry to consensual youth is a serious one because many of them become the oppressors of minority people and supporters of injustice, cruelty, and racism. This ministry is of grave importance because the danger facing oppressors is greater than the suffering of victimized people. The suffering of minority groups does not separate them from God but the sin of the oppressor does separate him or her from God.

A parent's or teacher's approach is not one of judgment if he or she believes that God has broken down the walls of hostility between all people. God loves the prejudiced as well as those sinned against. It is this love and acceptance made incarnate in Christ that a parent and teacher must also embody in his or her approach to consensual youth. As indicated, the approach is educational—confronting stereotypes, stimulating reflection, and clarifying the truth of God's grace.

6. Cry of the Joyous

It's a feeling, it's a knowing, it's a being . . . you can't define it really.
A seventeen-year old girl

Of the five cries of youth, one of the most insistent and frequent is the last in the series.

Joy pulsates through this fifth cry. It may take the form of quiet exuberance over the simple pleasures of living. Or it may be a shout of celebration and hope that contrasts with the despair and cynicism as often heard in the twentieth century. It is the cry of youth whose joy is in a sense of identity and mission that centers in the person of Jesus Christ. As a minority group (about one-third of all church youth) these youth exemplify in what they value, believe, perceive, and do the impact of identifying with a personal God and a believing community.

In short these youth have found a meaning system that brings order into their lives and gives answers to ultimate questions of existence. For them Christianity deals with the "really real" and supplies an explanation of "what life is all about." Their affirmation of faith, muted during the sixties, has become more audible in the ensuing decades.

Their joy does not always become clear in a single incident or at a first meeting. Instead snatches of conversation, several incidents, and moments of contact collect, and one day you realize that they add up to a cumulative portrait of lived-out faith, persistent joy, and hope.

Christine was like that. Not the most vivacious person in her youth group, she was often downright quiet. She was not the prettiest because, although she had lovely hair and a beautiful smile, she struggled with complexion problems. But I remember her with respect and pleasure. I remember her in a discussion session, leaning forward in her eagerness to be understood. "But nobody ever promised us a rose garden, Pete," she said to a boy who had just spoken. "Believing that God loves you doesn't keep things from happening and hurting you. I mean, boy! When my dad was sick for so long, we were really scared we were going to lose him—I mean I had some really bad times. But, see, having faith means that you know Jesus is in there, hurting and struggling along with you. It means you're never all alone. That's a *great* thing to know."

Her look of joyous certainty was familiar. It was the reflection of an understanding of life as a precious gift, to be savored, appreciated, enjoyed, and shared.

My memories of Christine are of her responsible concern for others and patient acceptance of their quirks and oddities. Most clearly I remember a kind of realistic optimism, a hopeful person with her eyes wide open.

Youth Who Have Found an Identity

One winter's night I sat at a table in a restaurant and chatted with a young man whose life had just been featured in a movie entitled *The Drug Scene*. It told the story of a high-school student from a middle-class home who became part of the drug culture of his community in California. His life became one of rebellion and complete separation from his high-school friends, parents, teachers, and pastor. After two years of drugs, including heroin, he was a shadow of the husky young man who once had held such promise of football prowess.

The night I talked to Mark Lindley he had fully regained his health and was looking forward to marriage and a career. What had made the difference? Through Christian friends he had been led to a commitment to Jesus Christ, and these friends formed a support group that sustained him during the painful months of returning to freedom and responsible living. A personal faith restored his life.

There is now a new interest in the power of a personal faith because of its evident impact on the lives of so many youth. Religious conversions are radically changing the lives of some drug addicts, moving them away from personal isolation or total involvement in the addict culture into communities of faith where they become truly human. Authorities are coming to acknowledge that a young person's chances of becoming a delinquent, suicide, or truant depend heavily on his or her religious orientation and participation and that of his or her family. Interest is growing in the way a religious faith affects more vital and responsible citizenry.

The power of religious faith to transform lives showed up in our 1984 study of young adolescents (ages ten to fifteen). When we singled out those for whom faith is central and important, we found more youth than average reflecting high self-esteem, love for their church, and the ability to say no to life-denying activities and yes to life-enhancing activities (Strommen and Strommen 1985).

This description of early adolescents echoes the cry of joy found in our analyses of 7,050 youth in 1970. At least 30 percent of the youth identify with a personal God, are active with God's people, and seek to grow and develop as Christians. Furthermore they feel morally responsible to God, want to help the suffering, and hold a hopeful outlook with respect to the future. These youth are committed to a life of faith and responsible living, representing a distinct facet of church youth. They are youth who reflect an attitude of joy and gratitude in being alive.

Overall they testify to intensity of religious faith and a desire to live responsibly. The youth described here are

identified with a personal God,
active with God's people,
motivated to grow and develop.

Identified with a Personal God

A dominant characteristic of believing youth is identification with a personal, caring God. It goes beyond assent to doctrinal statements, to affirming an experienced reality. It is declaring something intensely personal: "I am convinced that God hears me, cares for me, forgives me. I have been in his presence, I have the sense of being saved, I have been heard by God." Youth who experience these realities accord great importance to their faith; it is the primary inspiration of their lives. For committed youth Christianity is primarily a personal relationship. Though these youth are often confused on doctrinal matters and unable to distinguish between a humanist religion and the historic Christian faith, they feel identified with God. And this oneness with God is their source of joy.

Faith is like a kite above the clouds. You can feel that exciting tug every once-in-awhile—a reassurance that he is there.

Life in itself is a miracle and you get so excited sometimes, you flow with thanks!

Jane Larson, age eighteen

The impact of a personal faith shows dramatically when the ecumenical youth are grouped on the basis of answers to the question, "how important is your faith?" The biggest difference shows in belief about God and Jesus Christ. Of those who rank faith as "unimportant," only one-fifth believe there is a God; fewer believe that Jesus is the divine son of God. This contrasts with almost nine-tenths for those whose faith is "very important."

Youth's awareness of a personal, caring God correlates with the importance that they accord their faith. The young man whose faith is important to him feels quite confident that he has a personal relationship with God. He believes that God cares for him in a special way, that God hears his prayers, that he is being saved in Christ, that he is being forgiven by God, and that there is indeed a life after death.[1]

An identification with God is necessary for religious certainty. Though admittedly subjective this sense of God's presence permeates all of the young person's life, affecting attitude, behavior, and life goals. Without it the young person is adrift.

The survey indicates that, as subjective and hidden as this feeling is, it is visible in practical, lived-out behavior. The four

Figure 6. Characteristics of Committed Youth

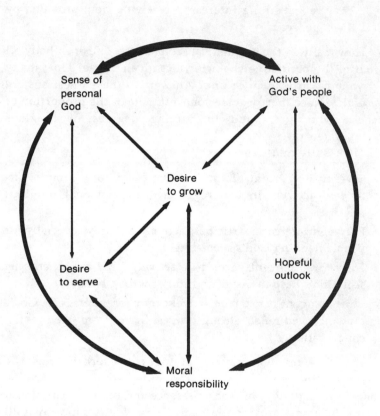

Heaviness of arrow indicates strength of intercorrelation.

most typical characteristics of youth who know a personal God are these:

1. They participate actively in congregational and private religious activities.
2. They pray especially for people needing God's special help.
3. They seek God's help in deciding right or wrong behavior.
4. They reflect strong interest in receiving help provided by the congregation.

How many in the ecumenical sample (N = 7,050) embody all four of the predictive characteristics given above? How many have only three, two, or one? Answers to these questions are useful because they provide some estimate of the proportion of youth who are found in varying degrees of religious commitment.

The results are these:

• Seventy-six percent of youth in the ecumenical sample participate actively in congregational and personal religious activities.

• Fifty-eight percent participate actively *and* pray especially for people needing God's special help.

• Forty-three percent participate actively, pray for others, *and* seek God's help in deciding right or wrong behavior.

• Thirty percent participate actively, pray for others, seek God's guidance, *and* reflect strong interest in help provided by the congregation.

The 30 percent who embody all four characteristics might be viewed as the most religiously committed youth. They are the ones most conscious of God's presence and the most convinced of his love and providential care. These youth, more than all others, are eager to grow in their faith, become involved in service, and be challenged. They stand in marked contrast to the 24 percent whose lack of interest signals a loss of faith.

Faith does not make all of life easier; a mature perception of

Christianity indicates that it isn't meant to. Our data shows that a religious faith raises concerns as well as alleviating them. Distress over everyday adolescent problems does not vary with intensity of personal faith. Those who profess a faith are as bothered over lack of self-confidence, academic problems, personal faults, classroom relationships, and national issues as those who do not.

The major impact of a personal faith is seen primarily in what young people believe, value, and perceive. It affects their ethical behavior, stated concern for others, outlook on life, attitudes toward parents and congregation, and sense of personal responsibility.[2] Notable in our data is the fact that "faith-is-important" youth and "saved" youth rank much higher in self-regard. Because feelings of worth are a vital ingredient in the life of an adolescent, this is an important difference.

Active with God's People

The Siamese twin of identification with a personal God is involvement in a religious community. The two highly correlating characteristics are like two sides of a coin, answering the questions, who am I? and, who are my people?

Involvement, as used here, means more than church attendance. It includes being part of a religious community (attendance, financial support, membership in a youth group), taking seriously its major emphasis (Bible reading, prayer, corporate worship), adopting its basic beliefs (in God and Jesus Christ), and feeling positive about what is offered (congregational life, youth activities, and family).

The importance of religious participation and its close tie with personal faith surfaces in a multivariate analysis known as Automatic Interaction Detection (AID). In this complex computer analysis thirty-nine possible predictors are analyzed simultaneously to determine what variables are most closely associated with saying, "My faith is important." Our analysis shows that the most powerful predictor of youth who see faith as "very important" is participation in the life of a congregation. Conversely the most powerful indicator of youth for whom faith is not important is little or no participation in the life of their congregation. In other words, dropping out of congregational life is strongly associated with a diminished interest in a religious faith. Lack of involvement in a community of faith powerfully indicates disbelief in the reality of God. Though the reasons given by youth for leaving their church may be valid, it is unlikely that they are the primary reasons for their disengagement from the congregation. It is more likely that their leaving signals a crisis in faith and unbelief.

How many youth are among the disinterested? If the answer is based upon interest in specific aspects of religious participation, then percentages will vary widely. Two-thirds of all church youth seldom, if ever, open their Bibles for private reading; nearly as many seldom, if ever, give any of their income (1 percent or less) to church or charity. Less than half report regularity of private prayer and participation in the church youth group. About one in five in the ecumenical sample seldom, if ever, attend church.

If all these indices of religious interest are combined into one category called religious participation, we find that one out of four in the ecumenical sample is disengaged from the community of faith and minimally identified with a personal, caring God. Three out of four touch base in some way.

For committed youth involvement in the life of a congregation is more than performing a series of religious duties or obligations. It is being a part of a subculture that reinforces faith. It is identifying with people who, in sharing the same faith, serve as a support group. Encouragement for this interpretation is found in the contrasting way of life (attitudes, values, behavior) of youth who attend church regularly (weekly or more often) as against those who do not attend.

What does church attendance indicate?

When the sample is divided on the basis of church attendance two contrasting cultures become evident. Most nonattenders favor gratification now (e.g., premarital sex, getting high on alcohol); most attenders are willing to delay gratification. Most nonattenders place little value on charitable giving, Bible reading, or taking one's religion seriously; most attenders encourage each other in these practices. Most nonattenders criticize their church and avoid activities that would involve them in helping others; by way of contrast most attenders are happy with their congregation and are likely to assist in helping activities.

Obviously cultures overlap; attitudes and beliefs that typify nonattenders are found also among some attenders and vice versa. But the point is that the climate of attenders is congenial and encouraging to committed youth, whereas the climate of nonattenders is hostile and discouraging to the religious person.

Attending church is more than an isolated event in the life of church youth. It is a tangible expression of identification with a community of faith. Most regular attenders have a sense of belonging, being known, wanted, or missed when they are absent. Many find their best friends at church and enjoy a sense of family when worshiping with the congregation. For them church attendance provides occasions for fellowship. It is no surprise then that high attenders reflect a strong sense of who they are in relation to the family of God, of knowing where they belong.

Most youth who attend church several times a week are happy with their church (73 percent), in contrast to only 20 percent of the nonattenders. Eighty-three percent of the regular attenders say, "When I attend worship services, I am among friends," as against 34 percent of the nonattenders.

Youth group members—losers only?

Some insist that youth who stay with their church, and particularly the loyal members of youth groups, are primarily "losers." They are variously seen as the "straights," the less interesting and prosaic ones. Some call them neurotics who, not being able to make it at school, huddle together in a church youth group for security purposes.

Though such generalizations may be on target for youth in

some congregations, they are not so for most church youth. Comparing the 55 percent who attend a church youth group more than one-half the time with the 45 percent who do not, we find identical concerns over family unity, parental relationships, life partner, lack of self-confidence, academic problems, and classroom relationships. They are identical also in maturity of values, humanitarian attitudes, and frankness. Though participants in church youth groups are more concerned over their personal faults, they still rank higher in self-regard. There is no evidence that one group can be pitted against another on matters of personal adjustment or feelings of low self-esteem.

Where the two groups part company is in areas related to religious commitment. Large score differences show that attenders are more

eager for help
conscious of their moral responsibility
conscious of a personal, caring God
positively oriented toward their youth group and church.

Slight but statistically significant differences make it possible to add that attenders are more

involved in social action and aspire with greater eagerness to a life of meaning and service.

Nonattenders are more concerned over national issues and more oriented to change.

In summary it is not true that regular attenders of church youth groups are less mature and more socially inadequate youth than nonattenders. If distinctions need to be made, they must relate primarily to religious interests. The distinguishing characteristic of youth who attend youth groups is the greater likelihood of religious commitment.

What are the strengths and weaknesses of today's church youth groups as perceived by the youth? If the ecumenical sample is a fair indication of church youth generally, we can say that church youth groups, compared to most organizations, have maintained a fair balance of boys and girls (46 percent boys, 54 percent girls). The youth enjoy being together and do reflect a fair esprit de corps. Primary weaknesses as perceived by the youth are these:

1. Fellowship does not achieve the depths where members feel free to truly share themselves and their feelings.
2. Too little is done to improve the group.
3. Too few participate actively.

Motivated to Grow and Develop

A third characteristic of religiously committed youth is their strong interest in opportunities for growth and development. They are eager to participate in a range of activities offered by their church, even if it means going out of their way to do so.

Do committed youth what help? To answer this question we singled out the 918 youth who most resemble the profile of committed youth. We found that they, more than others in this study, want opportunities for growth in faith and service. They are, more than the rest, open to educational experiences that will enable them to be in touch more vitally with themselves, others, and God.[3]

Well-meaning adults often plan youth activities with an unrealistic stereotype of youth in mind. They do not realize that there are subcultures within a congregation, each with its distinctive interests and needs. Religiously committed youth differ markedly from young people who are not so committed. This is why a diversified ministry is essential. What strikes fire for youth having one need hopelessly bores those with another. Interest in some activities is closely related to the importance youth accord their faith. Enormous differences in response characterizes the two groups. A youth ministry dares not plan for a hypothetical average or settle for a stereotype that assumes all youth have similar interests and needs.

Highly committed youth declare strongest interest in opportunities that will increase their faith and their sense of identification with God and the church. Of the top seven in preference, all but two are God oriented. First and foremost, these youth, sensitive to their relationship with God, covet opportunities to enhance their sense of the presence of God. They want an increased ability to speak cogently of their faith, coupled with a better understanding of Scriptures. Convinced of God's providence, they want help in discerning his guidance and coming to know a life of meaning and purpose.

The next ten items in rank are relationship oriented, as seen in table 15. The youth's choices witness to a strong desire to make friends and be friends, to do less public posing when in a group—to be more "the real me." Committed youth want the experiential learning found in groups where members are past playing games with each other and can speak candidly about what they think and feel. In addition to desiring honesty and forthrightness, they want their group to be an accepting and caring community that also includes fun and social activity. The quality of depth interchange is eagerly desired. One touches the interests and needs of the majority of committed youth when offering the opportunities described in table 15.

Inferred Needs

Are there emphases that ought to be considered over and above the declared needs of committed youth? Two that seem warranted from the data are the need for conceptual clarity and the need for orientation to change.

Cognitive clarity is not one of the dimensions that characterize religiously committed church youth in the ecumenical sample. Though they are enthusiastic about their faith, they are not able to distinguish the particularities. Though conscious of a personal, caring God who forgives them, they are not able to distinguish (cognitively at least) between a humanistic religion and historic Christian doctrines. They are as likely as uncommitted church youth to agree to statements of an American folk religion. Quite uncritically too the committed youth say they believe that "God is satisfied if you live the best life you can." They will assent to the statement "Although there are many re-

Table 15
What Highly Committed Youth Want Most
N=918

Activity	Percentage Declaring Much Interest
To experience a closer relationship with God	93
Meetings where I experience the presence of God	87
To learn to speak naturally and intelligently about my faith	86
Guidance in finding out what God's will is for my life	86
To learn how to make friends and be a friend	81
To learn to know and understand the Bible better	81
To find meaning and purpose in my life	80
To experience acceptance in a group of people who really care about each other	77
To learn to be more of the real me when I am with other people	77
Group meetings where people feel free to say what they really think and are honest about what bothers them	76
To learn how to be a friend to those who are lonely and rejected	76
To learn what a Christian really is	74
Recreation and social activities where youth get acquainted	74
To find a good basis for deciding what is right and wrong	72
To learn to get along better with members of the opposite sex	72
To learn about Christian views of sex, dating, and marriage	72
To develop greater ability to show a loving concern for others (both near and far away)	70

ligions in the world, most of them lead to the same God."

It is quite evident that ability to make theological distinctions is not a distinguishing quality of the youthful committed person. He or she is quite likely to equate Christianity with another religion, to reject a doctrine of original sin, to discount theological distinctions as "head trips," and to insist that Christianity is no more than living as Christ lived. (Here many will applaud the youth, depending, of course, on the importance they accord Christian truth.) Like new converts, committed youth are primarily occupied with their experience of release from guilt and loneliness through knowing Christ. A teaching that harmonizes with this experience is accepted as valid.

One naturally wonders if there is any indication in the data of resistance to change among committed youth. If so, what kind of change? First of all, they do not resist change relative to the social issues listed below. Here committed youth are as progressive in their desire for social justice and innovation as the uncommitted.

The students should have more to say about what is taught in my high school.

All war is basically wrong.

Every person has a right to free medical care if he needs it but cannot afford it.

Every person has a right to adequate housing even if he cannot afford it.

There are three changes resisted by committed youth: premarital sex, unwillingness to enter military service, and resistance to law enforcement. Of the three, change in attitudes toward premarital sex is the most adamantly opposed. Only 9 percent of the most highly committed youth agree that "sexual intercourse before marriage is okay as long as you love the other person." This contrasts with agreement from 35 percent of all others in the sample.

A second point of.resistance to change is in regard to military service. Seventy percent of the highly committed (N = 918) feel that every young man should be willing to serve in the armed forces. This compares to 55 percent for all others in the sample. Greater hawkishness does not seem to be involved, however, because identical proportions of both groups (two out of three) believe that "all war is basically wrong."

Change in attitude toward law enforcement is the third point of difference. Eighty-one percent of the highly committed youth believe America needs greater law enforcement, as against 67 percent of all others. This difference of 14 percent contributes to the negative correlation noted earlier, as does the opposition of more committed youth to radical student activities. Only 21 percent agree that "the protest of college students is a healthy sign for America." This compares to 37 percent for all others.

To conclude, committed youth are more conservative on some issues. In these areas one can expect a tendency to maintain status quo or resist change.

Finding a Way of Life

In a day of anguished alarm over what is happening in our society it is worth noting that the way of life of religiously committed youth flows out of convictions such as these:

I am morally responsible for the way I live and behave.
I find meaning in life through relationships with others and God.
I believe that God is active and that my future is in good hands.

Sense of Moral Responsibility

A sense of moral responsibility is strongly associated with both religious participation ($r = .53$) and a consciousness of God's presence ($r = .55$). This means, of course, that these characteristics of religious commitment are highly interrelated even though they are separate dimensions.

This interrelatedness is seen particularly when youth of the ecumenical sample are divided on the basis of the importance they accord their faith. The committed tend to look to God for help in making ethical decisions, whereas few of the religiously disinterested seek this help. For one group wrongdoing is ultimately sin against God, whereas for the other right or wrong is only one man's opinion.

Religiously committed youth tend to feel responsible for their neighbors. This feeling of responsibility is rooted in an awareness that one's final obligation is to God and that much of this obligation is lived out in relationships with people. The obligation is to live in an awareness of other human beings, always conscious of the purpose of life. It calls each person to a sensitive awareness of his or her own weaknesses and alerts him or

Figure 7. How Sense of Moral Responsibility Varies by Importance of Faith

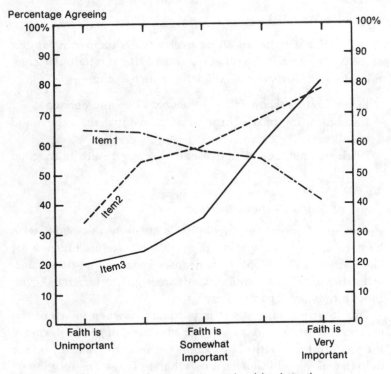

Percentage Agreeing

Item 1. What is right or wrong is only one man's opinion. (agrees)
Item 2. When a person wrongs his fellowman, he sins against God. (agrees)
Item 3. God helps me decide what is right or wrong behavior. (agrees)

her to the rightful place of self-denial and sacrifice. It causes him or her to believe that "God helps me decide what is right or wrong behavior," and "when a person wrongs his or her fellows, he or she sins against God." It causes him or her to disagree with the statement "What is right or wrong is only one person's opinion." This sense of moral responsibility rises and falls in relation to the importance one accords his or her faith.

The morally responsible person knows frequent inner battles.

Weighing alternatives and making choices is difficult, anxious work, but it is essential to the nature of morally responsible people. Youth know their battles well. The majority of church youth (ecumenical sample, N=7,050) agree that they are frequently torn between conflicting values, beliefs, and desires. One of their problems is not being sure enough of their beliefs when challenged by someone. However, if they believe something is wrong, half (49 percent) are convinced that a friend (boy friend or girl friend) could *not* persuade them to violate their conscience. The others are not so sure. One thing is certain: Church youth consider their beliefs highly determinative of what they will do.

There is a factual basis for this conviction. Current studies show that beliefs are the strongest predictors of what a person will do. In the study *Religion on Capitol Hill* (1982), Benson and Williams found that the best predictors of voting behavior of persons in Congress were these two: religious beliefs and political affiliation. Similarly, Search Institute has found that the strongest predictor of youth who will say "no" to premarital sexual intercourse is a moral belief, namely, that it is wrong. There is power in a person's beliefs and values. (Because religious orientation seems so closely tied to ethical beliefs and behavior, a closer look at issues such as premarital sex, drug usage, and excessive drinking is given in an extended chapter note.)[4]

Desire to Serve

Committed youth are especially intent on finding meaning in life through relationships with others and God. In this they resemble the 2,200 children of clergymen (college freshmen in 1969) who participated in the American Council on Education's Cooperative Institutional Research Program. PKs (Preacher's Kids) differed in some of their answers from the 250,000 incoming college freshmen of that year. They showed a greater religiosity than other students and less tendency to kick up their heels. More importantly both sons and daughters of clergymen were more oriented toward "service" fields, tending to reject the more lucrative and prestigious fields. A larger proportion than average were also politically involved. Sons of clergymen

(54 percent in the sample) were especially singled out for their more humanitarian attitudes and their devaluation of worldly success (Bayer and Dutton 1972).

When church youth rank their life goals, two ways of life or clusters of behavior emerge. One way of life places a high value on adventure, recognition, pleasure, personal freedom, and plenty of money. High priority is also given to personal power, personal physical attractiveness, and skill or expertise. All these are values strongly related to self-development. The second way of life values a life of service, responsibility toward others, meaningful work, wisdom, honesty, a relationship with God, getting and receiving love, and knowing forgiveness and family happiness. The tendency is toward a wider life orientation.

These two ways of life, or value orientations, characterize church members between the ages of fifteen and sixty-five. Values of self-development are especially attractive to 76 percent of fifteen- and sixteen-year-olds but remain attractive for only 50 percent of the twenty-three- and twenty-four-year-olds.

This suggests that self-development goals are linked to the normal process of developing a sense of worth based on personal power, recognition, skill, achievement, physical appearance, and personal freedom. Adventure, pleasure, and money can be linked to normal biological drives for creature comforts, exploration, and gratification of instinct.

Meaningful life

The person who endorses the cluster of life goals called meaningful life values relationships with others, service, ethical life, love, meaningful work, forgiveness, honesty, and family happiness. In short, he or she consciously endorses a value system in which meaning is found in relationships with man and God.

If all values in meaningful life are ranked as "least important" and all values of self-development are accorded "extreme importance," a theoretical score of 53 is obtained. If the priorities are reversed, a theoretical score of 146 is obtained. The higher the score, the more movement toward mature, meaningful values.

The average for all church youth is 115 (freshmen, 113; seniors, 118). The value system of this sample of youth points in the direction of purposeful living.

The value orientation shifts for those who consider personal faith unimportant, as indicated by a score of 107. The difference between them and the religiously interested who scored 120, translated into percentiles, is 30 percentile points.

Social action

We have already seen that youth today feel the hurt of their abused fellows. More important than concern is social action. What does a person do to express his or her beliefs and concerns? Significantly three out of four church youth try to reach out in a helping relationship to lonely and rejected youth. Three out of five spend time in a program of service to defend members of minority groups and raise questions about social issues. At least half give money to people in need, identify with the suffering of others, and discuss ways in which a Christian should relate to civil rights, aging, student protest, and war.

Admittedly there are many ways of demonstrating concern for others; there are motivations other than religious commitment for reaching out in a helping way. In this study, however, social action is positively linked to religious commitment through correlations with each of its dimensions. Though these correlations are not strong, they indicate that religious commitment is one of the motivating forces. For instance, we find that the more importance youth give their faith, the likelier they are to be involved in serving activities. With increased importance of faith goes an increased sense of being one's brother's keeper.

A Hopeful and Positive Life Perspective

Committed youth tend to view their church youth group and congregation positively, to hold themselves in high regard, and to feel hopeful about the future. These attitudes can be considered characteristic, along with God awareness, religious participation, interest in help, moral responsibility, and desire for a meaningful life.

The importance of hope, eagerness, and openness to the future is best evaluated against the disillusionment, despair, and basic distrust of twentieth-century people. It contrasts with the attitudes of low self-esteem youth who feel cynical about life, separated from themselves, others, and God. It opposes peers who distrust adults and criticize all institutions, who are disillusioned with life and look to the future with despair.

Are church youth generally hopeful?

A substantial majority take a positive view of the future. Almost nine out of ten believe that it is possible to make the world a better place in which to live. Eight out of ten, convinced that the future is more than a matter of luck, do look forward to becoming involved in activities that win their respect. Two out of three are convinced that good can come out of their problems and that there are many forces in life working for an individual. They have a sense of sharing in a great purpose. Feelings of joy and exhilaration about life characterize them.

Has the Cry Changed?

The cry of the joyous has changed slightly. Consider, for instance, the year 1977, when the 6,833 youth using the youth survey represented church young people. They gave evidence of a growing religious interest among church youth from 1970 to 1977. Our measures of the cry of joy showed a substantial increase in religious participation, in awareness of a personal God, and in self-esteem. Lacking, however, was any advance in youth's desire for meaningful service or an increased sense of moral responsibility.

In 1980 we saw the same advance in religious interest for Lutheran youth. Over the ten-year period (1970–80) a marked upturn occurred in the number aware of a personal and redeeming God, active in their congregation, and perceptive with respect to biblical concepts. But no advance appeared in youth's desire for meaningful service. Rather there was a statistically significant decline in the extent to which youth are involved in helping activities.[5] One sees in this decline a contrast to the other dimensions of this cry, evidence of the diminished interest in service that characterized the seventies.

Gallup and Bezella (1992) in their book, *The Religious Life of Young Americans*, draw attention to the spiritual interest of today's youth. Their findings show that most young people pray, believe that religion is relevant to the modern world and hold positive attitudes toward their churches' youth ministry. In fact, the authors report that youth are more likely than their elders to believe in heaven and hell.

The sobering side of this more optimistic picture appears in findings of the 1988 survey of high school seniors. Here one sees that one-half "rarely" or "never" attend religious services. Almost that many deem religion as of "little" or "no" importance in their life. And equally sobering, two out of three think their ideas about religion resemble those of their parents (Bachman et al, 1988, 18, 176).

If it is true that there is a growing spiritual interest among American youth in the nineties (and that seems to be true) it is paralleled by a diminished institutional involvement. What we have may be a more privatistic, non-involved religion. This is seen in a notable decline in the percentage of high school seniors who in 1988 attended religious services once a week or more. The drop is from 41 percent in 1976 to 35 percent in 1985, to 32 percent in 1988. This is a significant decline. Similarly, the number contributing financially to their church or synagogue dropped from 31 percent in 1976 to 26 percent in 1988. Clearly, the number of American youth involved with the ongoing program of a religious institution has diminished.

Though the numbers are diminishing, involvement for young people who do remain active remains a powerful stabilizing factor. When Search Institute compared youth actively involved in the life of a congregation with non-participants they found significant differences in their behavior. The congregationally inactive were twice as likely as actives to be involved in an at-risk behavior. To illustrate, 42 percent of inactive youth reported being sexually active as compared to 22 percent of active youth. The consistent findings are that a personal faith is a major force in the moral development of youth and for some the chief determinant (Eklin and Roehlkepartain, 1992).

The possibility of a growing self-centeredness with respect to the religious interest of American youth squares with the report of Oxford Analytica (1986) on American adults and religion. "Though the statistical indicators of religion are up, its social indicators are down. Today's radical individualism, psychological narcissism, and consumption revolution is eroding the vitality of today's religion" (p. 116). This statement implies that being preoccupied with one's relationship to God while ignoring suffering in society can result in a self-centered piety.

George Gallup, having noted that basic indicators such as religious preference, church attendance, church membership have remained basically stable over the years 1977–86, does, however, see clear-cut signs of renewed religious interest in the country. He notes an upturn in the number of Bible study groups and a new religious ferment on campuses. In a 1985 study for the Christian Broadcasting Network, Inc., he discovered that one-half of the nation's adults spoke of being more interested in spiritual matters now than they were five years ago (Gallup 1985).

His study of teenagers (ages thirteen to eighteen) in 1984 showed an increase over 1978 in their interest in and belief in the supernatural. The percentage of those believing in angels rose from 64 to 69 percent in 1984 (Gallup 1985). Symbolic of this shift toward enhanced religious interest is the cover title on the *Washingtonian*, December 1986, announcing "God is Back." Its feature article describes how Washingtonians, particularly young adults, are returning to religion.

Significant too is the discernible shift taking place in the moral values people embrace. Studies in 1986, particularly those of Yankelovitch, Skelly, and White, show a growing disenchantment with the philosophy that "anything goes." Their reports speak of an emptiness of soul and growing hunger for realities beyond reach of the physical senses. A new interest is emerging among adults and leadership youth in finding connections between the transcendent and one's daily life.

By 1987 a discernible shift had taken place in moral values.

Gallup reported a growing disenchantment with modern ways of life. The Yankelovitch polling service saw a new receptivity to discipline, authority, responsibility, and commitment. A return to something like basic American values, which could be labeled a new traditionalism was occurring. The group for whom this was especially true was the baby boom generation, now in their thirties and forties.

Interestingly this return showed up also with a select group of high-school seniors. Surveys of high achievers, those listed in *Who's Who of American High School Students,* showed the following trends over the past ten years, 1976–85:

an increase in teens who have never had sexual intercourse (78 percent)
an increase in teens who have never used drugs (80 percent)
a decrease of 30 percent over a ten-year period in males and females who approved of abortion.

I find it significant that during the past ten years the percentage of youth who agree with the values of their parents on eight different issues—religion, education, dress styles, friends, and so on—has gone up. To illustrate, the percentage agreeing with their parents on drug use has gone from 50 percent to 75 percent. I was amazed to see youth's answers when asked about censoring the media; 72 percent said they would censor media presentation of "explicit sex." Clearly a trend toward greater acceptance of universal moral values was emerging and with it an interest and willingness to view ethics as a public issue.

Viewed in context, these signs of intensified interest in spirituality and growing sense of moral responsibility may be harbingers of a new day of opportunity for youth ministries. They may presage an openness to the realm of the spirit, so intrinsic to the Christian faith. Studies of religious interest and beliefs since 1920 have shown a cyclical rise and fall over the past decades. Having bottomed out at a low point in the seventies religious interest seems to have entered a decade or two of strength.

Changes among Church Youth

The cry of the joyous seems to have intensified. Gupta's fifteen-year trend analysis (1970–85) shows a marked advance in youth's God awareness and religious participation. More youth in the 1985 sample are aware of a personal, loving God, and more are actively identified with their congregation. The advance is striking. Significant too is their gain in feeling morally responsible and viewing themselves with a higher sense of self-esteem.[6]

One dimension of commitment not showing an advance over the fifteen-year period is the measure of values, namely, a meaningful life. It suggests that the desire of youth to serve in 1985 is the same as that measured for youth in 1970.

This more optimistic data may raise questions about the adequacy of the 1985 sample. Regarding this, there is no argument. Though not a random sample of church youth, the survey is still a significant indicator of trends. Directions pointed by its data are the same as those established by the checkpoints of 1977, 1980, and the surveys of American youth in 1985. Indicators of a revived religious interest and a growing sense of responsibility reported by observers of the American society corroborate trends indicated by this 1985 sample.

The cry of joy has become more intense, indicating possibly a new day of religious interest for church youth and a new day of opportunity for youth ministries.

This at least is what it seems to me. We face a decade or two of opportunity that ought not be ignored. Why? Because every major denomination is losing a major segment of its youth. Now is the time to bend the course of history with respect to youth and reverse the trend of non-involvement. Now is the time to minister to their growing interest in spiritual experience.

Why the urgency? The 1990 landmark study of Protestant youth (*Effective Christian Education*) points up the need to rethink our present ways of passing on the faith in home and church. Measures of mature faith show no increase between grades 7 and 12 but rather a decrease (Benson and Eklin, 1990, 25, 65).

What can reverse this trend? More parents sharing faith in their home; more congregations making Christian education a high priority for both youth and adults; more service involvement of youth with adults; and more youth groups where the study of Scripture is at the heart of their fellowship activities. These imperatives will increase the number of youth who reflect a cry of joy.

The cry of joy that typifies one in three church youth is the overflow of a sense of identity and mission in life. Sometimes it is overpowering elation that breaks out in song; it is more usually the quiet confidence that "God walks with me, talks with me, and tells me I am his own." Its dominant characteristic is identification with a God who loves me and with a people who care about me. It is the feeling of being a whole person.

The six characteristics of committed youth show the inseparability of ethics and religion. Joined to the three characteristics of God relationship, religious participation, and interest in help from the church are three elements of an ethical life: moral responsibility, a caring attitude, and positive outlook. For committed youth morality is not determined by a public opinion poll; the ethical is not what most people do. Instead the ethical is a moral earnestness, an intentionality that includes caring for people. For these youth a Christian faith emerges as a positive moral force.

7. Reaching Out

You have listened to five cries and become aware of five distinct, though overlapping, groups of church youth. You have become attuned to five areas of need and sensitive to the way each can dominate a young person's thinking.

Though the five cries have been presented as comparable in importance and scope, it must be noted here that the first and fifth cries—self-hatred and joy—are the dominant ones. They emerge from the research (second-order factor analysis) as the most intensive, cohesive, and pervasive of the five. In them one meets a classic theme of alienation and reconciliation. The first cry is one of alienation from self, others, and God; the fifth is one of identification with God, his people, and their way of life.

This fact does not mitigate the urgency of the other three cries; it only stresses a priority. Estrangement from God, a characteristic of humankind, leaves one restless and unhappy. Until youth come to know God as a personal, loving Father, they experience varying degrees of cosmic loneliness. Whoever reaches out to these youth must understand the loneliness that often characterizes the psychological orphan, the angry humanist, the unreflective bigot, and even the committed Christian.

The Issue of a Cosmic Loneliness

Mary had been talking quietly for a long time, exploring questions about herself, her family, her life. "Sometimes I look at the stars and think how far, far away they are, and how much there is going on in the world—in the whole universe—that I don't know anything about. Then I feel awfully little—kind of nothing—but yet I know I'm not.

"Sometimes it's kind of scary just to be alive in the middle of all that. I wish I could be as sure as other kids seem to be about where they are and about what's right, and about God really being close by and helping when you have a mess in your life to work out. I'm not there yet, where I can be sure about God. I would like to be, but I'm not.

"Well, maybe that's phony, too, because I'm not sure I always would want to be asking what God wanted, if that makes sense. Because I like to see if I can do things on my own too.

"Some kids seem to be able to think mostly about the future as being important. I keep hearing kids say, 'I'm going to be this. I'm going to be that,' but it's never 'I'm this now.' What is scary to me is the feeling that I'm never going to lose the feeling that I'm going to be ... later on. Why isn't it important what I do now and what I am now?"

Mary, with her sense of being "in the middle of all that," voiced the longing of many to find wholeness and significance in an overwhelming universe, to find it now. She reflected a basic lonesomeness for God, a wistfulness coupled with an admiration for friends who had found a confident faith. But lonesomeness was matched by a desire to flee God, to be her own god, order her own life.

This ambivalence issues in a longing for God, mingled with fear of a God who speaks through one's conscience. The cry is one described by Augustine, "You have made us for yourself, O Lord, and our hearts can never rest until they rest in you."

In one large denomination 63 percent of the youth report some degree of apartness from God and man; one-half of this group gave evidence that for them it is an acute issue. They are anxious about their relationship with God.

"I do not feel close enough to Christ."
"I wish I could have a deep faith in God."

They feel isolated from people and the excitement of life.

"I feel all alone in the world fairly often."
"I often feel as if it would be good to get away from it all."

They lack a sense of purpose; they feel that life has no meaning.

"In thinking of my life I often wonder why I exist."
"I have discovered no mission or purpose in life."

Anxiousness about God, a feeling of isolation from life, and a sense of purposelessness are indicators of a cosmic loneliness that found words in the verse Nancy wrote in her green notebook:

> Words have many meanings
>   especially my own
> when people come to see me
>   I often turn to stone
> for when the puzzle is fitted
>   the pieces off the floor
> the picture can be recognized
>   and torn apart once more
> for in my tiny castle
>   I often sleep quite sound
> when nothing's there to bother me
>   and no one is around
> but when the winter's ended
>   (time to go and play)
> I wish that there was someone
>   that I wouldn't chase away.
>   Nancy Nelson, age seventeen

Adults underestimate the extent to which youth are anxious about a religious faith. They assume that young people are unperturbed over their relationship with God, casual about feelings of guilt, and unconcerned with doubt. Actually these are among the most disturbing thoughts of youth.

In the ecumenical sample used in this study almost half (43 percent) the respondents strongly wish they could find a deep faith in God, and the same proportion are "much bothered" because they do not feel close enough to Christ.

A Point of View

Sociologist Andrew Greeley, in his book *Unsecular Man: The Persistence of Religion* (1972), establishes a case for a person's need of an ultimate interpretive scheme that can give his or her life form, order, and direction. He argues that modern people, faced with persistent and overriding bafflement, even in a supposedly scientific and rational world, are caught in despair. Young people who do not know who they are, where they are going, or why they live reveal in exaggerated forms a widespread listlessness, apathy, discouragement, and frustration (Greeley 1972, p. 260).

I find in my studies the same despair and sense of alienation among youth and adults who lack a faith. When we singled out the secular, change-oriented skeptics in *A Study of Generations*, we found this same note of despair. These liberal rejecters of a faith tend to view life as meaningless, are least able to face life or death, and of all of the adult group are the most anxious about their apartness from God. The need of youth and adults for a vital Christian faith is no less strong today than it was in the past. Questions about ultimate reality continue to demand an answer.

A poignant illustration comes in the words of Brigitte Bardot, the sex symbol of the sixties. At thirty-eight she has become a recluse with little interest in life. The Associated Press quotes her as saying, "I hate humanity. I am allergic to it. I see no one. I don't go out. I am disgusted with everything."

Unfortunately despair is often expressed in ways that increase the alienation. Many drug users and sexual adventurers, needing the warmth and affection of close relationships, try shortcuts. They experiment with their lives, looking for satisfactions that can come only with knowledge, maturity, and personal commitment.

Girls can score just as many times as boys if they want to. I've gone to bed with nine boys in the past two years. It's a natural thing, a nice thing and a nice high. It sure can clear up the blues.

Mimi, eighteen years old

My father was always gone, and I think my mother expected too much of me. She couldn't understand, and I couldn't explain. . . . You walk around with suppressed emotions and you've got to get them out. That's the fascination of drugs; they get you out of yourself.

Bob, twenty years old

The American belief in instantaneous solutions is as widespread as the air we breathe. It is often assumed that complex mental, moral, or spiritual processes can be completed instantaneously. Tragically the use of drugs increases this conviction.

Most despairing people believe that maintaining long-range ethical ideals is impossible or at best foolish. They do not expect future fulfillment nor do they value what lies in the future; the present moment and their current needs are overwhelmingly important.

The person who feels alienated from life is not able to postpone immediate pleasure for the sake of future gain. Like many poor people, he or she sees little value in setting goals for the future because of the unlikelihood of achieving them. Without a vision of the future delay of gratification makes no sense. The despairing and alienated youth needs an answer to the question, what are the real values that are worth waiting for?

Peer-oriented Youth

The quality of life described above intensifies the cries of self-hatred, family conflict, social protest, and prejudice. The youth for whom this is especially true are primarily peer oriented. They tend to distrust adults and take their signals from their own age group, in contrast to broadly oriented youth, who trust adults and relate well to people of all age levels.

Our studies show that a disproportionate number of peer-oriented youth hold themselves in low esteem and take a negative view of life and especially of adults. Some, psychological orphans of parents who have driven them to find refuge with their own age group, are peer oriented more through parental fault than through a preference for their own age group.

Other peer-oriented youth have left the "straight world" for ideological reasons. They break with tradition out of protest against the way institutions perpetuate social injustice. Others seek to escape from excessive rules and regulations; their primary goal in life is freedom from authority and imposed standards.

For others the cause is loss of faith; in despair over not finding meaning in life they choose self-destructive paths. In *A Study of Generations* we found that 18 percent of the church youth were peer oriented, being both antiadult and antichurch and to some degree involved in the life and attitudes of a counterculture.

Our data tells us that the most likely candidates for a counterculture are those who feel low self-esteem, who are pressured at home, concerned about social issues, overregulated, and alienated from God. It also indicates that, though studies of American youth in 1970–71 show a strong generational consciousness and a tendency to identify with their own generation, peer-oriented church youth are a minority.

Hannsen and Paulson made a study of 210 twenty-year-olds. Half of them (N = 116) were antiestablishment subjects drawn from a random sampling of youth who entered the Los Angeles Free Clinic, a medical facility and gathering place for antiestablishment culture. The other half (N = 94) were university establishment-oriented and "straight."

The two groups contrasted strikingly in their relation to organized religion. The disaffiliation rate of the antiestablishment group was 88 percent as compared to 15 percent for the establishment youth.

How Effective Leaders Approach Youth

How does one reach out in a helping relationship to the youth described in this book? The people best qualified to answer this question are youth leaders who themselves excel in reaching out. In order to hear what they say we first had to locate the cream of the crop.

Through a study conducted in 1970, we developed criteria for effective youth leaders. Once the criteria were ranked we asked the heads of national youth organizations to nominate leaders of high-school youth who exemplify some of the highest ranked criteria.

Ninety-one youth leaders were named by the following groups: American and Southern Baptist (10); Roman Catholic

(6); Christian Church (9); Church of God (9); Evangelical Covenant (7); Episcopal (4); American and Missouri Synod Lutheran (21); United Methodist (6); Greek Orthodox (2); United Presbyterian (1); and Young Life (16). The ninety-one workers then told, through questionnaires, why they intervene in the lives of youth, how they approach them, and what accounts for their effectiveness.[1]

Motives

The first of three questions put to the workers was, why do you intervene in the lives of young people—that is, what contribution do you feel that you can make to their lives? As might be expected, over half the respondents cited religious motives: "I want to share my faith," "I can guide them to a full Christian commitment," and the like. Virtually all, in some part of their free responses, used a desire to influence youth in directions consonant with the Christian way of life as their predominant motive. And this motive clearly arose out of love, concern, and profound respect for youth.

Many responses showed that the leaders were keenly sensitive to the autonomy of youth and committed to techniques that would not violate it. Thus they did not speak of evangelizing youth, controlling their environment, supervising their behavior, preaching the gospel to them, or other tactics that might be interpreted as applying pressure. Instead they made statements such as "I can listen," "I can communicate," "I can be a friend," "I can be a significant adult in their lives," and "I can share my happiness."

A number of insightful youth leaders also recognized that their motivation includes self-realization. "They contribute to my goals." "They keep me young." "I can learn from them." But there was no evidence of self-aggrandizement at the expense of youth, only self-fulfillment as a consequence of helping others develop their potential.

Methods

Three questions were directed to the skills exercised by successful church youth workers. The first question was, what ways of approaching youth have you found helpful? (How do you get next to them?) Responses revealed six groups of skills:

1. Building Relationships
   Knowing them—home life, school, friends
   Exhibiting deep, sensitive, personal concern for them
   Showing them courtesy
   Participating with them as an equal
   Showing appreciation for a job well done
   Helping them if they ask
   Sharing mutual experiences
   Sharing my own feelings about life
2. Being Genuine
   Being adult
   Speaking in my own vocabulary
   Being honest and open
   Stating my convictions while leaving freedom for theirs
   Boldly speaking out in radical situations
   Admitting I don't know all the answers
   Dealing with my own hang-ups first
3. Being Available
   Going to their events when adults are welcome
   Spending time with them and their friends
   Working and playing with them in various activities
   Taking kids to "away" games
   Inviting them to my home for dinner
   Initiating interviews
4. Showing Interest
   Remembering their names
   Learning about their world
   Being able to speak their language
   Listening to their music
   Adopting their symbols
   Finding areas where I can be of help
   Phone calls and letters regarding their accomplishments, interests

5. Communicating

Talking to them every opportunity I get

Slow, quiet listening; waiting for the chance to say some things

Listening with the third ear for emotions

One-to-one counseling

6. Leading

Discovering and using their talents and interests

Involving them in planning, decision making and executing activities

Letting them find their own thing and do it

Accepting their decisions

Facing them with the issues

Holding unpopular positions that I think are best for them

Giving them provocative, challenging books

Offering them a host of options

Presenting a better alternative by the way I live and act

Getting them interested in trips, projects, studies to benefit them

Creating celebration and experiences for free expressions

Getting them to camps, retreats

The second question asked of this group, "what are you doing to accomplish [your] purposes [with youth]?" revealed three new groups of skills:

7. Teaching

Training others to reach out on a one-to-one basis

Training leaders to program "exposure events"

Reeducating adults for helping roles with youth

Teaching the Scriptures, presenting verbally and non-verbally the message of the love of Christ

Teaching a class relating Bible, youth, and culture

Personally confronting each youth with the claims of Christ

Relating youth's ideas to Christian faith
8. Creating a Community
Helping them to get to know each other
Encouraging group awareness and sensitivity in every-
day life
Finding Christ in each other, in everyone we encoun-
ter, in everything we do
Through involvement, making them aware of loneli-
ness, deprivation, friendlessness
Helping forgiveness and acceptance to happen
Developing teamwork among youth in their activities
Trying to build a staff community
9. Encouraging Involvement
Involving kids where they can grow, experience, relate,
share—volunteer work, seminars, schools, inner city,
community
Service projects in other localities
Getting young people into congregational life
Creating opportunities for kids to think about, talk, act
out their concerns
Discussing issues and trying to do something about them

The final question was, "if you were to describe the secret of
your effectiveness, what are some of the ways of working with
people that you have found effective?" It elicited no skills beyond those already revealed, but some new illustrations
emerged for the eighth skill, creating a community: "developing groups who share at the deepest possible level" and "keeping the group open to friends of church youth."

Helping Youth into a Life of Faith

Research on Religious Development, a review of research literature on the religion of youth (1900–69), established that adolescents who have direct personal experience of the presence of
God differ from those who do not. Our study shows in what

ways they differ: outlook on life, relations with people, motivation, and sense of moral responsibility. It demonstrates that relationships with God, man, and self are inextricably linked. This is why a personal faith is deemed important by those who have it; it is why a parent will ask, "How do you help a son or daughter know a personal, caring God?"

A fitting answer is given by leaders in Young Life, an international youth organization, who underscore the necessity of first taking the time to establish a relationship of love and trust. Once an open and cordial relationship is established, questions of ultimate significance begin to surface. "I don't know what I would do if God didn't exist. But does he?""Why doesn't he make it easier for us to believe?"

The Searching Questions

It is natural for adolescents to feel that their faith depends upon themselves, that they have to "make it" with God. And so they ask, "Am I good enough?"

Assuming the negative answer, they conclude that "God is not interested in me." Added to this concern is youth's fear of losing the respect of admired adults. Some are embarrassed to admit to parent or pastor that they struggle with doubts and question some things they have been taught. Mingled with these feelings is the wistful, unvoiced question, "how do I 'get' faith?"

When the Bible is quoted its words become enmeshed in the quicksand of further doubt. "The Bible was written for people centuries ago. By what stretch of imagination can I assume that it speaks to me? How do I know that interpretations I make (or you make) are correct ones?" How can the words of the Scriptures ever be windows through which one sees an invisible God? Finally, because youth respond as total people, illness, depression, fatigue, or the pressure of circumstances tend to increase their feelings of religious uncertainty.

Times of Reflection and Decision

Youth retreats, informal discussions in a home, and personal conversations provide choice occasions for helping young people think through their relationship with God and voice both their lonesomeness for God and their desire to flee him.

At times like these young people, preoccupied with standards of right and wrong, come to recognize an issue deeper than the matter of sins per se. It is the question of authority: Do I remain the captain of my ship, or do I acknowledge the love and authority of the God who created me?

During times of reflection and decision youth need the freedom to discuss the mystery of their rebellion and their proneness to go it alone. One can only encourage them to remain open to God's voice, allow times for listening, and take advantage of moments when he can be heard. These are not times for a hard sell or for "thought-terminating cliches" that can force an artificial conversion that is mere acquiescence to a religious culture, without knowledge of the love and grace of God.

Youth need to understand that Christianity is a relationship with Christ, in which doubt is admissible because one relates to a person and not to a set of doctrines. Accepting a personal, caring God comes first; in coming to know him one learns what is embodied in propositional truths.

When youth hear what God has done in the past and can do again for them, conversations about God become hope-inspiring occasions. Youth's attention shifts from themselves and their problems to the promises and possibilities of the Christian faith. The emptiness of a lonely life and the drawing power of love implicit in God's promise motivate them to enter God's possibilities as a child returns to a parent's arms. In receiving a Savior youth come to a personal transcendental experience with Jesus Christ.

A Supportive Congregation

A personal faith needs the sustaining power of a group. But what can give youth a sense of welcome and identification with his congregation?

Of the thirty-nine possibilities tested, two were highly associated with positive, warm feelings toward one's congregation: the first, to feel that one fits in well with some group in the congregation; and the second, to feel inspired at worship services. It is hard to overemphasize the identification youth feel with their congregation when they are secure in a small group. If the youth interact freely in discussion groups of twelve to fifteen people, they later find the freedom to share themselves in the larger group.

An enigma for youth is why gatherings to celebrate their faith, such as Sunday morning worship, are often dull. Many find inspiration totally lacking in this function of their church family.

Unlike adults, youth today are conscious not only of God's transcendence but also of his immanence. They look for more than a service that stresses his holiness, transcendence, and awe-

Table 16
Percentage Inspired by Local Worship Services
Ecumenical Sample
($N = 7,050$)

	Percentage Saying Yes
Never inspired, only bored	11
No longer inspired, but I once was	11
Very often inspired	13
Quite often inspired	17
Sometimes inspired	32
Seldom inspired	11

some greatness. They want more than the solemn beauty of a service where architecture, music, and liturgy create the sense of God's presence. Youth also want to worship the God who sits next to them in the fellowship of believers.

Youth want to worship a Christ, not only divine but also human, who is a part of rhythm, melody, and ordinary speech. They want a service that inspires, encourages, and helps them to feel what they are unable to make themselves feel.

One group of youth, after several weeks of discussing the issue, agreed on three things they want in a morning worship service. First, it should be a time of singing, of expressing happiness over what God has done and is doing. If a service does not lift one's spirits, why speak of good news? Second, they want to learn something new and be stimulated intellectually by fresh insights into Christian truth. Third, they want to participate and meet God in the presence of others. They want the service to impart a sense of warmth, love, and community.

A Stance toward Youth

Though this book is written for parents and youth leaders, it should not be assumed that adults have outgrown youth issues. On the contrary, the preceding analyses show how much adults are linked to youth needs.

Low self-esteem is probably passed on from parents.

Family disunity centers in parental conflict.

Social concern is characterized by youth's sharp criticism of congregational adults' lack of manifest caring.

Prejudice is found more readily among adults than among youth.

Loss of faith is an issue that is no respecter of age.

A ministry to youth is best seen as a collaborative effort—mutual seeking, helping, and working—in which adults freely admit their need to be helped in ways similar to youth. To believe that "no one has arrived" enables everyone, regardless of age or experience, to express the need for rebirth or renewal, for judgment and forgiveness.

The stance of common need reduces the age prejudice that characterizes most adults and mitigates the generational chauvinism of youth who feel superior to adults in such personal values as openness, honesty, and feeling for people.

It does not require that young people be seen as little adults. One can still view adolescents as possessors of special qualities—liveliness, enthusiasm, honesty, idealism, and potential—and rightfully say, "I enjoy them," "They keep me young."

The preceding chapters draw attention to at least two imperatives in a youth ministry—*mutuality* and *mission*. Youth of all subcultures want the warmth of an accepting group, which is *mutuality*. They need activities that give them a sense of purpose; that is *mission*. To achieve these imperatives *educational experiences* are needed for youth and adults that open minds, develop skills, clarify values, and encourage commitment.

Notes

1. To Hear and Understand the Cries

1. Less than 2 percent of published studies concerning the impact of psychosocial variables on health include the religious variable. Larson (1983) reviewed articles appearing in four major psychiatric journals (1978–82) and found only 59 of 3,777 quantitative studies reported included religious variables. Most of the 59 studies limited their assessment of religion to a single item, such as denominational identification or frequency of church attendance. The same percentage (2 percent) was found in a review of all published research back to 1940 (Strommen 1969). One can conclude that this pattern characterizes the research literature (Buehler, Hesser & Weigert 1976).

2. When the correlations of youth's answers to the 420 items were analyzed, the items formed twenty-five clusters. These in turn were subjected to a second-order factor analysis in order to derive the five sets of characteristics.

3. The five sets of characteristics (factors) that provide the structure and documentation for the chapters of this book are listed here. The nature of each group is established by the characteristics that load most heavily (i.e., highest numbers).

Factor One — Low Self-Esteem

Positive Loading

87	Personal Faults (concern over)
81	Lack of Self-Confidence (concern over)
79	Classroom Relationships (concern over)
64	Academic Problems (concern over)
61	God Relationship (concern over)
58	Life Partner (concern over)
51	Lack of Family Unity (concern over)

Negative Loading

−52	Self-regard

Factor Two — Family Conflict

Positive Loading
73	Family Pressures
66	Parental Relationships (concern over)
63	Lack of Family Unity (concern over)

Negative Loading
−51	Family Social Concerns (perception of)

Factor Three — Social-Action Orientation

Positive Loading
69	Human Relations (Humanitarian Attitudes)
62	Orientation for Change
59	Involvement in Helping Activities
46	National Issues (concern over)

Negative Loading
−42	Congregational Adults as Caring (perception of)

Factor Four — Closed-Minded

Positive Loading
42	Family Social Concern (perception of)
40	Congregational Adult Caring (perception of)
36	Church Youth Group (perception of)
33	National Issues (concern over)

Negative Loading
−61	Biblical Concepts
−30	Human Relations (Humanitarian Attitudes)

Factor Five* — Religious Commitment

Positive Loading
82	Religious Participation
79	Awareness of a Personal God
68	Interest in Help
67	Sense of Moral Responsibility
54	Desire for Meaningful Life
54	Church Youth Group (perception of)
44	Congregational Adults as Caring (perception of)
43	Involvement in Social Action
32	Self-Regard

---

*Though listed here as the fifth factor, it follows Factor One in strength and intensity.

4. Our data provides additional information about families of church youth as well as information on school and leisure-time activities.

Family

In the ecumenical sample three out of four youth (78 percent) report that both parents belong to the same congregation and nine out of ten say that at least one parent belongs to a church. The religious earnestness of these parents is not known except to say that in 14 percent of the homes family devotions or prayers are held regularly.

One-fourth (26 percent) of the main wage earners are in a profession (doctor, lawyer, teacher, minister, etc.), and three in ten (29 percent) are in sales or business activities. In addition to these white-collar workers 20 percent are in skilled or unskilled manual work, 6 percent in farming, and 4 percent in a service occupation (e.g., barber, waiter). New occupations, technical or scientific, account for 14 percent. These percentages indicate that more youth in the ecumenical sample come from white-collar homes than do youth in the total population of American teenagers.

This difference in socioeconomic status is reflected also in the educational level of the parents. Fifty-one percent of the fathers and 41 percent of the mothers have had at least some college or university work. This is well above the average of 24 percent for Americans aged 35 to 44, 19 percent for Americans aged 45 to 54.

Families of church youth are larger than the national average, with half the youth in the ecumenical sample reporting three or more brothers or sisters. No more than one in ten is an only child. The families are well established in their communities; no more than 15 percent have moved during the past five years. (Note well: the high mobility rates for Americans are related to age: 46 percent of Americans ages twenty to twenty-four move annually and also 38 percent of the twenty-five to twenty-nine age group. In 1969–70, 18 percent of all people in the United States changed residency.)

Stability of home life is shown by the fact that a majority of the church youth do not report difficulties and stress in their homes. Divorce or separation is known by one in ten (8 percent), and frequent illness by only 10 percent. Around three in ten of the youth (29 percent), however, are conscious of financial troubles in their homes, and about as many report serious difficulties such as prolonged illness, unemployment, death, injuries, or personal problems. Around one in four have trouble getting along with father (27 percent) or mother (25 percent), and 21 percent acknowledge that father is seldom home. In 43 percent of the homes mother is employed one-half to full time—a percentage similar to the national average.

School and leisure

Over half the ecumenical sample describe their grades as above average (42 percent) or excellent (11 percent). Less than one in ten admits to below average (7 percent) or very low grades (2 percent). Church youth have the ability to do well in school. Apparently they have the motivation as well; three out of four are never absent or at the most miss school once per month.

The ecumenical sample has a higher percentage (24 percent) than average of youth who attend a religiously sponsored parochial school. Private and technical schools account for another 7 percent, leaving a total of 67 percent who attend a public school. Only 1 percent are dropouts.

When it comes to leisure-time activities averages become misleading. A fifth of the youth (18 percent) are gone five to seven evenings per week from their home, and the same number are seldom gone (one evening or less). Though television is readily available, only one in five (20 percent) watch TV sixteen hours a week or more, and they show similar profiles to those who seldom watch it. If excessive TV watching constitutes a problem, it ranks in significance well below the issues posed in this report.

5. Margaret Mead contends that events between 1940 and 1970 have ushered in a new age. Today's youth, she says, are natives of this new world and are to adults like the advance guard of an invading army— strangers. She believes that between generations a break has occurred that is wholly new to history—a break that is planetary and universal.

In general Margaret Mead distinguishes three kinds of culture:

postfigurative, in which children learn primarily from their forebears
cofigurative, in which both children and adults learn from their peers
prefigurative, in which adults lean also from their children

Postfigurative Culture

According to Mead, this is the isolated, primitive culture where one finds three generations: grandparent, parent, and child. One rears his or her children as he or she was reared; teaching what he or she was taught. The underlying assumption is that youth accept unquestioningly what is unquestioned by the adults. As a result there is considerable conformity to, and replication of, the past.

I was conscious of three-generation families when visiting Norway in the summer of 1971. In the homes I visited the grandparents were honored people whose opinions were respected. They served as links to the traditions of the past and gave the children a sense of history. If there was generational tension, it showed in youth's reactions to their parents.

Co-Figurative Culture

In the co-figurative model both children and adults learn from their peers. Contemporaries are the strongest influence on individual behavior, whether this behavior involves adults or youth. The style of life and the limits, however, are established by adults. It is a pattern of life where people of two generations share with each other.

Co-figuration occurs when the experience of one generation is radically different from the preceding generations, as when youth emigrate to a new land and encounter new situations and new ways of handling them. Youth of this culture, though reared to expect change, understand that it is change within the changeless. It is assumed that in spite of the change they will retain their cultural identity, and everyone knows and agrees on basic values. In such a culture it is possible for radical groups to become champions of the past and to institutionalize their values. One can assume that in the co-figurative culture there is tension between the past and the changing present.

This pattern may exist in church life where adults collaborate with youth in partnerships in which co-seeking, sharing, and co-working are mutually enriching.

Prefigurative Culture

In Mead's opinion today's youth are part of a new culture. Underlying this view is an assumption that nothing in the past is meaningful or workable and that one can learn very little from adults.

This new culture proclaims that existing social structures must be torn down to make way for radically new approaches to critical world problems. Social bulldozing is required, says Margaret Mead. It is assumed that adults cannot teach *what*, but only *how* to learn. Youth do not want to be told *what* to be committed to, but only the value of being committed to something.

In this culture a relationship of trust between adults and youth must be established along with a new way of life. Though adults will be needed to supply the know-how and stability, the youth can point out the needs and opportunities for building cooperation.

Mead believes that primitive societies and small religious ideological groups are primarily postfigurative; that great civilizations like ours have adopted co-figurative learning as a technique of incorporating change; and that we are entering a period, new in history, in which the young take on authority in their apprehension of the unknown future.

We tested Mead's "radical break" theory by using statements taken directly from her writing in a survey of Lutherans ages fifteen to sixty-five, *A Study of Generations.* If her claims that today's youth are a new breed are correct, we can expect that Lutheran youth will choose quite exclusively the statements of a prefigurative point of view. Also we can expect adults to reject prefigurative statements and choose only co-figurative or postfigurative points of view.

Postfigurative

Life is unchanging and will continue largely as I know it.
The accumulated wisdom of the past should be one's primary source of learning.
Young people learn primarily from their forefathers and elders.
I have accepted unquestioningly what was taught by my elders.

Co-Figurative

Though life is constantly changing, human nature and human ideals do not change.
What is currently being discovered and what men have learned in the past are about equally important to learn.
Young people learn primarily from participating with adults and youth together.
Conflict and change have forced me to rethink and restate ageless truths for myself.

Prefigurative

Life has changed so radically that youth and adults cannot understand each other.
The past is such a colossal failure that there is little or nothing from the past worth learning except know-how.
Young people learn primarily from their own age group (peers).
I have questioned everything from the past and, together with my own age group, have sought new approaches to life.

Approximately two out of three youth preferred co-figurative to prefigurative responses. The same proportion of adults also preferred a co-figurative position. Only 21 percent of the youth, ages fifteen to twenty, chose the prefigurative statements, as against 15 percent of the adults, ages thirty to sixty-five. The difference of 6 percent is too slight to be significant, and certainly does not warrant talk about a radical break between these generations.

If, on the other hand, we see Mead's typologies as world view that are favored by one age group more than another, then we have supporting, though weak, evidence. Most likely to agree to postfigurative statements are people fifty to sixty-five years old (19 percent), and most likely to agree with prefigurative statements are the youngest, ages fifteen to eighteen (24 percent).

One can look at Mead's theory as a prediction of the future and consider it an interesting hypothesis. Viewed in this light, her analysis is both provocative and instructive. We may, in fact, see more of the prefigurative mode in the years to come. A shift in perceptions, values, and attitudes toward adults may be in process. But there is little evidence that such is the case now, at least as far as church youth are concerned. To talk about a new breed when referring to this population is to propound a myth.

2. Cry of Self-Hatred

1. A separate sample was drawn of young people who most resemble the profile of low self-esteem youth. They score in the top quarter on personal faults and lack of self-confidence and in the lowest quarter on self-regard. The penetrating quality of loneliness became apparent through a multivariate analysis (Automatic Interaction Detection) of the data. This method was used to identify the elements in a young person's life that most powerfully predict self-esteem (the scale, self-regard, being used as the dependent variable). Thirty-nine possibilities were examined simultaneously to determine which accounted for the most variance of self-regard. Of the thirty-nine possibilities used as independent variables, the one ranking first was the item "I tend to be a lonely person"—meaning, the most powerful predictor of youth who hold themselves in low regard is their admission of continuing loneliness. Ranking second to loneliness was the statement, "I sometimes consider suicide." This means that when the dimension of loneliness is controlled (i.e., its effect or impact is kept constant), thoughts of self-destruction are most indicative of low self-regard.

2. Unpublished paper presented at the International Congress of Learned Societies in the Field of Religion, Los Angeles, California, 1972, by Drs. Peter Benson and Bernard Spilka, University of Denver.

3. Figure 8 shows how the population of 7,050 youth divides when analyzed by means of an AID (Automatic Interaction Detection) program. Thirty-nine contributors to low self-regard were processed si-

multaneously against the dependent variable, self-regard. This process locates the most powerful predictor of self-regard (the dependent variable). Having divided the sample on that predictor, it locates the second strongest variable and divides the sample again. The three items contributing most to self-regard (and which, therefore, can be called predictors) are these:

1. being less critical of oneself
2. not considering suicide
3. enjoying high grades

The strongest predictors of low self-regard (in order of importance) are these:

1. being highly self-critical
2. considering suicide
3. considering one's faith unimportant

The concept of esteem may not be measured simply by isolating one dimension, self-regard. Therefore another analysis was carried out using self-criticism (personal faults) as a primary focus. Again a multivariate analysis was used to determine the proportions of youth who report high or low self-esteem.

Of thirty-nine possible contributors to a self-critical attitude, the two most powerful predictors turned out to be high concern over classroom relationships and extreme concern over one's lack of self-confidence. Using these as prime indicators of low self-esteem, we can say that one out of five (20 percent) are troubled in these ways. This is identical to the percentage that resulted when self-regard was used as the basis for the multivariate analysis.

4. Dr. Daniel Offer began his studies in 1962, collecting data over an eighteen-year period from normal adolescents, using the Offer Self-Image Questionnaire. This instrument, standardized to gather information about the phenomenal-self of teenagers, was administered to high-school students primarily of the middle class. In the early sixties the survey of 130 items was given to a representative sample of students at three suburban public high schools in the Chicago area. In the late seventies it was given to subjects choosing to cooperate on a research project. These subjects were found in ten high schools, public and parochial, located in rural, suburban, and urban areas. Because the samples of the two decades differ in type, location, and economic level, the differences Offer reports in adolescents of the two decades may have occurred for reasons other than self-image.

5. This is a good comparison. A national survey of all students in

Figure 8. Major Predictors of Self-Regard

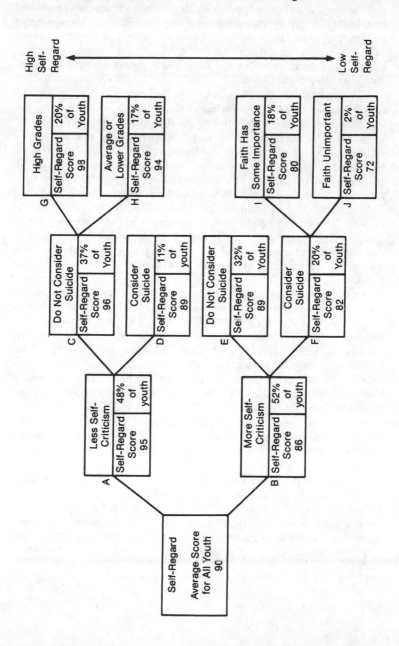

Lutheran parochial schools of the Lutheran Church–Missouri Synod was carried out in 1979 using the Youth Research Survey. A 1980 report on this study did separate the students into two groups: Lutheran and non-Lutheran. Using scores of the 3,340 Lutheran students, we can make a comparison with the 1,900 Lutherans who took the same survey in 1970. Though this latter group was not randomly chosen, its average scores approximate those of the 7,050 youth on whom the survey instrument was standardized.

6. The percentages found in table 5 are the responses of approximately 3,000 seniors sampled from approximately 125 randomly selected schools, a subsample within the national sample of 16,000 seniors responding to the items found in table 5. Since 1945 the Institute for Social Research at the University of Michigan has been making national surveys of seniors in public schools to monitor trends in the way of life and values of American youth. Results of their annual surveys are published each year in a document entitled *Monitoring the Future,* by Lloyd D. Johnston, Jerald G. Bachman, and Patrick M. O'Malley. The publisher is the University of Michigan's Institute for Social Research.

7. The five dimensions of self-hatred for which a trend analysis is possible are measured by scales that average .84 in reliability. This means that for samples of the size used here we have fairly precise measures.

The comparison between scores from 1970 and 1985 was made in this way. The average of all scores from each scale in 1970 was compared to the average of scores on comparable scales in 1985, using students' "t" statistic scores. Here are the values of "t": family unity, 5.70; lack of self-confidence, 3.93; personal faults, 12.04; classroom relationships, 7.45; God relationships, 13.94; and self-regard, 20.64. All differences are significant at a .01 level. You will note that mean differences are especially large for self-regard, and well above youth's concern over God relationships and personal faults.

The trend indicated here parallels the slight advance found for American youth. The greater advance of church youth on self-regard may be due to the more select nature of the 1985 sample or to a stronger emphasis in congregations on a more affirming, gospel-oriented message.

8. Parent Effectiveness Training is a course in which parents learn the essentials of good two-way communication. Its founder, Dr. Thomas Gordon, heads Effectiveness Training Associates, a nationwide network of professionals offering training programs for parents, teachers, counselors, youth workers, and organizational leaders and administrators. Headquarters are located at 110 South Euclid Avenue, Pasadena, California 91101.

Further description of PET is found in chapter 3, chapter note 7.

3. Cry of Psychological Orphans

1. The predictive power (actually 35) of the item "My father and mother do not get along" is due in part to the fact that the item is also a part of the scale, family unity, that serves as a dependent variable. Table 17 shows other powerful predictors of family disunity.

Table 17
Predictors of Family Disunity

Item	No. of Times More Predictive of Family Disunity than Is Separation or Divorce
My parents do not trust me	19
My parents nag me	16
My parents try to pry into my private life	16
My parents do not understand my dating problems	16
My parents do not let me make my own decisions	15
It is hard to discuss my problem with my mother	14
My parents are too strict	14
My parents seem to have forgotten how it feels to be young	13
I have trouble getting along with father	12

2. A multivariate analysis using thirty-nine predictors with the family unity scale as the dependent variable identified the three most powerful predictors of Family Unity. Figure 9 shows how the population of 7,050 youth divides on the basis of three variables: parental accord, parental trust, and open communication. Concern over family unity drops from an overall average score of 46 to 36 to document the change in climate when parents get along. It drops again (indicating less concern over unity) to 29 when the second predictor, namely, parental trust, shows its influence by dividing the sample. Though third in rank, the importance of open communication is also evident in the scores. For youth who find it hard to discuss their problems with mother, the concern over family unity score moves up from 29 to 35.

3. Parents involved in helping activities enjoy homes marked by unity, good parent-youth relationships, and a minimum of pressures. The

opposite is also true. A consistent negative correlation varying between .30 and .33 exists between family social concerns and the other three family characteristics (family pressures, parental understanding, and family unity).

4. The standardized "t" scores that indicate the actual differences between the mean scores of 1970 and 1985 are as follows: family unity, 2.73; and parental understanding, 2.43. Both differences are significant at a .01 level. However, they are relatively modest in size.

5. All contrasts that compare adolescents of intact families with those found in stepfamilies, adoptive families, and single-parent families are significant at a .01 level. These differences could not have occurred by chance more than once in a hundred times. The self-reports of adopted adolescents (item 2) were also significant at a .01 level.

6. Peer Counselor Training is a highly effective fifteen-lesson course developed by Dr. Barbara Varenhorst, 350 Grove Drive, Portola Valley, CA 94025. Her program, developed fifteen years ago for students in the Palo Alto school system, is effective in teaching adults how to listen, communicate, and relate to others in helpful ways.

7. In Parent Effectiveness Training (PET) classes parents are taught to differentiate situations in which the child is having trouble meeting his or her own needs as a person and those in which the child is making it difficult for the parent to meet his or her own needs.

Parents are given skill training in those forms of verbal communication shown to be most effective in helping another person overcome difficulties in meeting his or her own needs. They are actually taught the particular forms of communication utilized by competent professional counselors, such as "reflecting feelings" or "active listening" (from Carl Rogers and other client-centered therapists), empathic "open-ended questions," and methods of keeping the responsibility for problem-solving in the hands of the child.

They are taught ways to modify the child's behavior that is interfering with the parents' needs. These methods have low probability of producing guilt and resistance and high probability of maintaining the other's self-esteem. PET thus teaches parents to send "congruent" messages (from Rogers), to be "transparently real" (from Sidney Jourard), to confront the child with "I feel . . ." messages, and to keep the responsibility for the problem with the parent who actually owns it.

Another aspect of training concerns specific methods of preventing conflicts between parent and child, such as enriching or modifying the child's environment, preparing the child ahead of time for change, and conducting participatory decision-making meetings for setting rules and policies that will govern the child's behavior in future situations.

Figure 9. Predictors of Family Unity

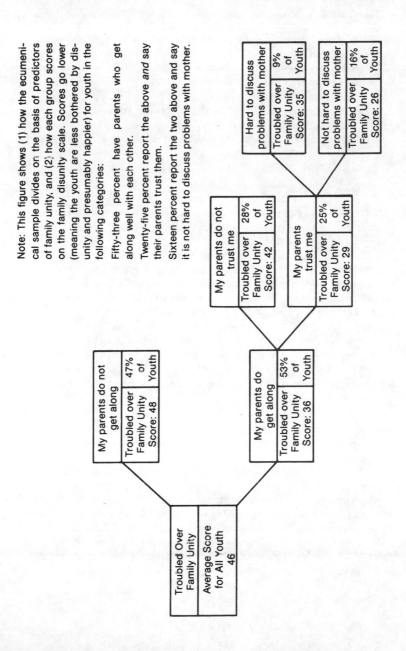

Note: This figure shows (1) how the ecumenical sample divides on the basis of predictors of family unity, and (2) how each group scores on the family disunity scale. Scores go lower (meaning the youth are less bothered by disunity and presumably happier) for youth in the following categories:

Fifty-three percent have parents who get along well with each other.

Twenty-five percent report the above *and* say their parents trust them.

Sixteen percent report the two above and say it is not hard to discuss problems with mother.

Hard to discuss problems with mother

| Troubled over Family Unity Score: 35 | 9% of Youth |

Not hard to discuss problems with mother

| Troubled over Family Unity Score: 26 | 16% of Youth |

My parents do not trust me

| Troubled over Family Unity Score: 42 | 28% of Youth |

My parents trust me

| Troubled over Family Unity Score: 29 | 25% of Youth |

My parents do not get along

| Troubled over Family Unity Score: 48 | 47% of Youth |

My parents do get along

| Troubled over Family Unity Score: 36 | 53% of Youth |

Troubled Over Family Unity

| Average Score for All Youth | 46 |

Throughout, parents learn the harmful effects of using either of two "win-lose" (power struggle) methods of conflict resolution—Method I (parent wins and child loses) or Method II (child wins and parent loses). A nonpower, or "no-lose," method of resolving conflicts is taught in which parent and child mutually search for an acceptable solution, making it unnecessary for the parent to force submission on the part of the child (Gordon 1970).

8. Youth-Reaching-Youth, known as Project YOUTH, was conducted by Youth Research Center, Minneapolis, under a grant (#MH17615-01) from the National Institute of Mental Health.

9. The program especially successful in developing a strong support group and effecting the discussed changes, is available in the publication *PEER Program for Youth*, by Ardyth Hebeisen, Augsburg Publishing House, Minneapolis, 1973.

4. Cry of Social Concern

1. The sample of 335 socially concerned youth was drawn from those who scored in the top quarters of the human relations, orientation to change, and social-action scales.

2. Gupta was able to assess three of the social concern dimensions in his analysis of trends over a fifteen-year period. He found that youth's responses in 1985, when compared with those of 1970, resulted in negative differences here presented in the form of student's "t" scores: concern over national issues, 23.64; orientation for change, 2.77; human relations, 2.06. The first two are significant at a .01 level and the third at a .05 level. The drop in concern over national issues (e.g., poverty, pollution, injustice, violence, nuclear warfare, and so on) is a remarkable one. It represents a drop of over .6 of a standard deviation, or roughly an equivalent drop of 23 percentile points.

5. Cry of the Prejudiced

1. The nature of the religiosity of the committed and consensual orientations may be more specifically inferred from the defining characteristics of each coding component. Briefly the individuals in the committed group conceptualize religion (content) largely in terms of abstract principles, intangible ideas, and relational expressions. They seem to order these concepts and express religious ideas with relatively clear meaning and nonambiguous referents (clarity). They also apparently distinguish and delineate a relatively large number of religious categories, characteristics, and functions using multiplex rather than

global or overgeneralized ideas (complexity). Such individuals further order these complex, abstract religious concepts discerningly and express their religious ideas clearly (clarity), examining and considering different or similar opinions, beliefs, and practices in a straightforward manner. This indicates an open and relatively accessible religious outlook (flexibility). Religion, for this group, is a matter of personal concern and central attention; the emotional commitment to religious ideas, ideals, and values seems to account for, or at least be relevant to, daily activities (importance).

By contrast the religiosity of the individuals in the consensual group appears to be more tangible and literal. Practical, observable referents and concrete, graspable images are preferred to abstract, philosophical ideas (content). Their view of religion is apparently vague, obscure, and indistinct in meaning and reference as reflected in "conventional" statements, vague generalizations, and amorphous, subjective impressions (clarity). While their religion is composed of a relatively small number of categories or elements, these are typologized and global with a tendency to use dichotomous or bifurcated categories and to evidence "two-valued" logic (complexity). Such a religion is relatively restrictive or closed to differing ideas and practices in that these individuals apparently try to narrow or encapsulate religiosity by rejection and distortion or by an "insistence" on appropriate ideas, proper behavior, and "right" beliefs. Such intolerance of diversity may also minimize perceived differences within their own belief system as well as generate a nonaccessibility through various "screening" techniques (flexibility). Lastly the religion of such individuals tends to be detached and neutralized. While considered important, it appears severed from substantial individual experience. It might also reflect an emotional "clinging" or magical quality or be neutralized and attenuated by other concerns or lack of positive affect and identification, thus rarely influencing or being involved in daily activities and behavior (importance) (Allen and Spilka 1966).

2. Age and education are strongly related to prejudice. A careful charting of their effects on church members from ages fifteen to sixty-five is found in *A Study of Generations* (Strommen et al. 1972, p. 209). Prejudice scores, lowest for youth, tend to rise with advance in years. However, graduate-trained adults, including clergy, do not score higher with age until they reach age fifty.

3. In *A Study of Generations* a major finding was the discovery of a prominent life orientation to rules and regulations among church members. A profile of this orientation consists of sixteen characteristics, of which the following are the most dominant: These people can-

not tolerate change, have a need for religious absolutism, are prejudiced, are threatened by people different from themselves, are self-seeking in their relation to religion, and believe in salvation by works.

These characteristics parallel the classic theological descriptions of a *law*-oriented person. Therefore we assume that the underlying quality uniting the constellation of sixteen characteristics can be called, in theological terms, a law-orientation.

An illuminating treatment of prejudice among church members is contained in James Dittes book, *Bias and the Pious*, published by Augsburg Publishing House, Minneapolis, 1973.

4. Distinctions made by Dr. Paul Holmer, Yale Divinity school.

6. Cry of the Joyous

1. The God-awareness scale, a dominant dimension in the factor of religious commitment, served as the prime indicator of religious commitment. A computer analysis ran thirty-nine independent variables against this scale, or dependent variable, to determine what contributes most to youth's awareness of God as a personal, caring father. The purpose is to determine the relative impact or contribution of each of the thirty-nine variables. The four contributing most are singled out as the most powerful predictors of a high or low awareness of God as a personal, caring father.

The analysis shows that 30 percent of the youth in the ecumenical sample can be classified as committed youth, with the rest of the youth reflecting varying degrees of religious commitment or the lack of it.

The unique contribution of this approach to data analysis is twofold: (1) insight into the structure underlying youth's awareness of God; and (2) an estimate of the proportions of youth found in each subcategory. Here are the conclusions on degrees of religious commitment that seem warranted:

1. Three out of four (76 percent) of the ecumenical sample (N = 7,050) are sufficiently involved in the life of their congregation to be identified as churchmen and -women.
2. Of these, 18 percent are not given to praying for others in need of God's help. Their diminished identification with God is symbolized by some (6 percent) who do not believe in a personal God. They are youth who participate actively in their church but lack a personal identification with God.
3. More than half the youth (58 percent) are involved in their congregation and pray for people needing help.
4. Of these a total of 15 percent do not seek God's help in deciding

what is right or wrong behavior: some (2 percent) because they do not believe in a personal God and others because they are not sufficiently conscious of God to be seeking his help. A few may consider it none of his business.

Here, too, are active churchmen and -women whose sense of a personal God is vague and unreal.

5. Two out of five (43 percent) church youth are keenly aware of God's presence (God-awareness score = 116). They pray for others in need of help and seek God's guidance as to what is right or wrong.

6. The most religiously committed youth are the 30 percent whose heightened awareness of a personal, caring God is reflected in their score (119) and in their strong interest in congregational activities.

7. Somewhat less committed youth are the 13 percent who take their faith seriously but seldom participate in the supplementary offerings of their congregation such as group meetings, youth activities, and special meetings. They show little or no interest in opportunities for growth and development and are less conscious of God's presence and help (score 110).

8. There are varying degrees of piety and confusion among the non-participants (24 percent) in a congregation. A third (8 percent) will admit to praying for others in need. The others who are not so inclined (16 percent) have among them a number who reject the idea of a personal God. But oddly, even among these there are the contradictory few (3 percent) who still seek God's help in deciding what is right or wrong behavior.

9. Among church youth a hard core of 5½ percent consistently reject a personal God. Four independent measures show that their alienation from God is both conscious and unequivocal.

10. Religiously committed youth are ones who are involved in a community of faith; pray for people needing God's help; seek God's aid in deciding what is right or wrong behavior; show interest in opportunities for growth.

2. Table 18 shows how declared importance of faith relates to dimensions of values, beliefs, and perception.

3. To determine the top-ranked interests of committed youth the following procedures were used. All who scored in the top quartile of three dimensions (God-awareness, religious participation, and moral responsibility) were singled out as religiously committed youth. The following discussion on help wanted by highly committed youth is based upon the percentage of these 918 youth who said, "I am very much interested and would go out of my way to participate" in this ac-

Table 18
Relative Importance of Faith

Scale No.	Dimension	Average Standard Score		Difference* in Standard Score
		Faith Important	Faith Not Important	
10	God relationship	50	45	5
11	Interest in help	53	43	10
14	Moral responsibility	53	43	10
15	Meaningful life	53	44	9
16	Religious participation	55	38	17
17	Social action	52	45	7
18	Self-regard	52	47	5
20	God awareness	54	40	14
22	Youth group vitality	52	46	6
23	Adult caring	52	45	7
24	Family social concern	52	46	6
		N=4,208	N=761	

*All differences are significant at a .001 level.

tivity. (Note: A fairly strong association has been found between declared interest and actual participation. Also it has been found that these items separate the religiously interested from the religiously disinterested youth. Highly motivated religious youth—for example, youth group officers—usually tend to choose many activities and declare strong interest. On the other hand, youth who rarely attend a religious service choose very few.)

4. Use of the three topics of premarital sex, drug usage, and excessive drinking does not mean that moral responsibility is no more than avoiding intercourse, drugs, and alcohol. The 1973 Watergate trials involving perjury, theft, invasion of privacy, and dishonesty of highly placed people reminds us that far more is involved. What follows is being shared because it is available data and because it shows how a sense of responsibility in matters of gratification is related to a faith commitment.

Church youth and premarital sex

Well over half (56 percent) of the ecumenical sample of 7,050 young people are bothered to some degree because they allow their feelings to affect their values in matters of sexual behavior The battle of conscience, however, is more than keeping one's feelings under control.

For half the population of church youth the problem is also a matter of being able to explain what they believe and why. They find it hard to defend their moral beliefs, to explain why they believe premarital sex is not okay even when it is an expression of love.

Statistics do not give answers to moral issues, but they can describe the youth who hold certain moral beliefs. Some who believe that premarital sex is okay reflect exemplary credentials. They know a sense of purpose in life, believe they are "saved," are concerned about others, are active in their congregations, chaste while on a date, devout, and conscious of God's guidance. These, however, are a small minority. The much larger number reflect a stance toward life that is antithetical to Christian commitment. They tend to have beliefs, values, attitudes, and ways of life that are self-serving and hedonistic.

The interrelationship of this belief with an unwillingness to delay gratification is seen when the sample is divided on the basis of response to the statement "As long as you love the other person, sexual intercourse before marriage is okay." The percentages given below indicate the number for whom sexual intercourse on a date is something considered possible—that is, an issue that poses a personal battle.

Of those who respond to "Premarital sex is okay"		This percentage will consider sexual intercourse on a date
Strongly disagree	34	4
Disagree	32	10
Agree	23	24
Strongly agree	9	37

Similar increases appear when the issues are drug usage, getting high on alcohol, or theft.

Premarital sex is okay	Have Used Drugs	Sometimes High on Alcohol	Have Taken Things
Strongly disagree	6	16	42
Disagree	11	27	51
Agree	22	47	64
Strongly agree	37	56	69

These youth favor chastity but possibly for different reasons than those of past years. The fear-oriented approach of yesteryear is giving way to more positive and goal-oriented controls. Young people are thinking in terms of the people they wish to be. Delay of gratification makes sense if it does not interfere with one's relationship to God or achieving one's purpose. Many tend to believe that the future can be trusted to provide sexual gratification in a marriage relationship. For them purpose and hope rather than fear of punishment provide the basis for delaying sexual gratification.

Another powerful inhibitor of gratification is the expectation of the community of faith to which the young person belongs. Bettleheim, in *The Children of the Dream*, notes the power of unspoken expectations in a Jewish kibbutz. Though housed in coed quarters and told that sex is natural, children sense very early the adult belief that sexual promiscuity interferes with the work and mission of the kibbutz. The expectation of sexual continence, based on community experience with unbridled promiscuity in early years, sharply limits youthful sexual involvement.

A community of faith provides the support group youth need for living in accord with their beliefs; the norms of congregation and home powerfully reinforce a youth's decision to delay sexual gratification until marriage.

American youth and premarital sex. A fair estimate of the attitudes of American youth toward premarital sex is found in Benson's study of 48,000 public school students (grades 6–12) drawn from 111 communities in 25 states. When asked if it was against their values to have sex while a teenager, only 24 percent of the boys and 46 percent of the girls said yes. When asked "Have you ever had sexual intercourse ('gone all the way,' 'made love')?" only 33 percent of the seniors said no. For most of these seniors, sexual intercourse was not a once-only experience. A total of 52 percent reported having had sexual intercourse 4 or more times. Of these only one-half protected themselves with some type of contraception.

It is significant that for 15 percent of these youth premarital sex begins while they are still in sixth grade. A sharp increase in percentage of those involved sexually mounts sharply between 9th and 12th grade (Benson, 1990, 86 and 88).

Among church youth, in 1990 (*Effective Christian Education*), the picture is not as alarming. The number of juniors and seniors who report never having had sexual intercourse is double the number of public school youth. And the percentage having had sexual intercourse involves only half as many. Clearly, one sees in this contrast the stabilizing influence of belonging to a community of faith. Sorenson in his study sees a trend when he observes that "adolescents are having sexual intercourse at an earlier age than before, and bringing less maturity and less rationality to bed with them." He also takes note of the ease that permits a female sexual adventurer to believe she loves any person she willingly sleeps with; she is apparently able to move in and out of love quite rapidly without confusion or remorse.

Sorenson's interviews showed that mutuality and belonging are emphasized by many young people when describing what love means to them. But they distinguish between a durable love (lifelong and rewarding to family life) and transient love, in which only intense love and a desire for sex are relevant. Such love, whether mono- or multi-affectional, is viewed as existing only for a time, for mutual gratification, with no commitments being made to the other.

The report further indicates that youth view sexual activity as a form of communication, a way of accepting another and in turn feeling accepted. Enhanced relationships rather than physical experiences are identified as most important to the youth of Sorenson's sample:

They look to their sex partners not for what the years ahead hold for each other but for what life has to offer today. Even a single intimate interlude offers comfort and solace to many adolescents; their commitment involves what each can mean to the other at the moment. The values to be realized by such a relationship may not be as enduring or deeply felt as those enjoyed by many married couples, but some self-realization is accomplished in sharing a sexual relationship with another (Sorenson 1973, p. 409).

The relationship between loneliness and premarital sex is seen especially in the youth singled out as sexual adventurers (those who seek many sexual partners). Sorenson found that, of all the sexual behavior groups he studied, sexual adventurers are most in conflict with their parents. Many do not feel they have gotten to know either parent; 58 percent of all sexual adventurers feel they have never gotten to know their fathers, and 40 percent believe they have never gotten to know their mothers.

The study concludes that premarital sex is not immoral in the eyes of most young people. For them sexual activities have no relevance to morality except in the way the activity is used. The objective is intimacy and warmth without any obligation or responsibility. For a large number it is sex without commitment, gratification without obligation, and transient love without promise. Significantly, Spilka, Hood, and Gorsuch in their 1985 book, *Psychology of Religion*, are able to demonstrate the inhibitory effects of religion on premarital intercourse. An added comment also seems appropriate.

We have had premarital and co-marital sex for nearly as long as man can remember with less than spectacular results in deepening the relational values that give significance to human life.

Eugene Kennedy

Drug Use

In our study we found that loss of faith is more strongly associated with drug abuse than parent-youth tension or low self-esteem.

This conclusion is based on an analysis of the 14 percent of the ecumenical sample who, in 1970, admitted to one of the five types of usage listed below. Other surveys in 1970 showed that up to 20 percent of American youth sometimes used drugs. It is not the percentage of use but rather the insight into characteristics and needs of users that is important here. No reference will be made to heroin users because the sample is too small and unrepresentative to warrant generalizations about church youth. However, Gorsuch and Butler do show the inhibiting effects of religion on initial drug abuse (*Psych. Bull. Review,* 1976).

Following are some of the conclusions that can be drawn from our data on church youth and that are supported by other studies.

Type of Usage	No. of Youth	Percentage of Sample
Use pot (marijuana) occasionally	511	7
Use pot frequently	162	2
Use pot frequently and have used acid (LSD)	143	2
Have used speed, either alone or with other drugs	115	2
Have used heroin or other hard narcotics	39	1
		14

—Drug users come from less cohesive families than nonusers; they come from homes where parents take a negative stance toward life and themselves. A notable increase in parent-youth conflict occurs when the usage moves from occasional marijuana to speed.

—Drug users are impulsive, with a high tolerance for risk; many have low self-esteem, often disguised as braggadocio.

—Drug users tend to form only superficial friendships, using the ritual of drug use to effect a sense of community. Fewer are identified with God or a congregation, shunning opportunities for growth, service, responsibility, and a life of purpose.

—Drug users are more skeptical about life and mix rebellion and cynicism when relating to home, school, and church. Fewer are positive about their families or congregations.

—Though they agitate for social justice, drug users are more prejudiced and less involved in social action than nonusers.

—Drug users of high-school age are more apt to exhibit low school performance and delinquent behavior. The majority favor premarital sex and getting high on alcohol (e.g., 70 percent of occasional pot users versus 25 percent of nonusers).

The close tie between drug usage and loss of faith suggests that religious commitment is, for many, the way of release from drug abuse. Psychotherapy ranks below a religious approach in freeing drug addicts. Teen Challenge, for example, approaches drug addiction as a moral disease and confronts youth with the possibility of release through a religious commitment; their record attests to the ability of religiously committed youth to shoulder moral and ethical responsibility.

Admittedly factors other than loss of faith are also involved in drug abuse. Addiction is frequently associated with the lack of an effective father figure during childhood; there is a high correlation between indulgent mothers and addiction in their sons. But whatever the causative factors the therapy that rehabilitates addicts features two ingredients: helping the person to a personal faith and supporting him or her through a sustaining community. The National Commission on Marijuana and Drug Abuse reported a direct tie between youth's feelings that life has no meaning and their use of drugs. The members of this commission see the growth and development of an ethical system as a necessary solution to the problem of drug abuse.

A striking contrast between church youth and nonchurch youth in regard to drug use comes from a 1970 study of students in a midwestern liberal arts college. Donald Chipman (Providence, Rhode Island, Drug Dependency Treatment Clinic 1972) and Clyde Parker (University of Minnesota 1972) began reviewing fifty studies of college drug-use patterns. They found that the national rate for marijuana "ever used" is between 40 percent and 50 percent. Since few studies classified students by extent of drug use, Chipman and Parker divided their random sample of eight hundred students into four groups: (1) regular users of marijuana; (2) casual users; (3) experimental users (e.g., tried it once or twice); and (4) nonusers. They found that the four groups were distinctly different in some areas and quite alike in others.

The most striking contrasts were between group one (regular users) and group four (nonusers). Group one members did not attend church frequently, if at all, and held a wide range of nontraditional as well as agnostic beliefs. Nonusers attended church regularly and espoused traditional beliefs about the supreme deity. Following are other controls:

Frequent Users of Marijuana	*Nonusers of Marijuana*
Highest use of strong and dangerous drugs	Little use of drugs (except in diet pills)
Highest alcohol usage and, for some, a problem	Least use of alcohol

Frequent Users of Marijuana	Nonusers of Marijuana
More active politically	Least active politically
Most critical of father's upbringing	Least critical of father's upbringing
Lowest grades	Highest grades
Most who feel estranged from their families	Fewest who feel estranged from their families
Most cynical about life	Least cynical about life

The authors identify the nonusers as the most distinctive of the four groups. Members of this group appear well adjusted, show confidence in what they are doing, and are willing to deal with life as they find it. The high correlation between religiosity and nonusage confirms our findings on the probable impact of a personal faith on youth's way of life and world view.

Drinking

Despite the furor over marijuana, cocaine and other drugs, alcohol remains the drug of choice for American teenagers. Close to one-half the seniors in a public school will have been drunk (i.e., five drinks or more in a row) at least once during a two-week period. This abuse of alcohol is also widespread among Protestant church youth. When asked if they have ever been drunk during the past 12 months, a total of 42 percent of junior and senior boys said "yes". Even more surprising, 46% of the girls acknowledged the same. Though Protestant youth may not drink to excess as often as American youth in general, this at-risk behavior is clearly identified also with them.

The reason for fewer drinkers among church youth is well known (Sebald 1972, p. 42). One's religious culture plays an important role in shaping attitudes and behavior relating to alcoholic beverages. This is seen in the percentage response of youth, when divided by denomination, to items about drinking.

The higher percentage of nonabstainers among Roman Catholic youth (19 percent) relates to the lack of official injunction against drinking among Catholics. Among Methodist and Southern Baptist youth, denominations in which most of the clergy oppose or condemn drinking and total abstinence is seen as an expression of moral earnestness, the number of abstainers is nearly half (49 percent).

Table 19
Drinking by Denomination (1970)

Item	Meth. N=522	Episc. N=529	Cath. N=1,818	Y.Life N=1,397	S.Bap. N=917	A.Bap. N=1,038
			Percentage Answering Yes			
I drink alcoholic beverages						
Never	49	24	19	25	49	35
Once a year or less	17	15	13	16	15	17
Two or three times a year	16	23	22	21	13	23
About once a month	9	20	22	19	12	16
About once a week	5	13	16	11	7	7
More than once a week	2	4	8	4	4	1
Blank	3	1	1	4	1	2
I sometimes get high on alcoholic beverages	18	34	41	37	22	23

Though the use of alcoholic beverages is inversely related to the importance youth accord their faith, there is a significant minority of religiously committed youth who do drink.

	"I sometimes get high on alcohol"
My faith is unimportant	53%
not too important	45
somewhat important	38
quite important	28
very important	22

These are youth who reject regulatory principles and prefer their own experience as the basis for deciding their norms. Their commitment is not to a system but to a way of being. They are determined to make only those decisions that build confidence in one another and sustain trust between persons. This may or may not result in total abstinence.

For many church youth, however, drinking is associated with less interest in personal faith. Our study indicates that youth who are sometimes high on alcoholic beverages and those who are not show greatest score differences on dimensions relating to religious commitment.

This extended treatment of moral responsibility may look as though the hallmark of Christianity is delay of gratification. It is not. A sense of moral responsibility involves a life of integrity and concern for one's fellow humans that bespeaks a life of love. These accents in the life of the committed are highlighted in the two remaining characteristics.

The significance of the previous pages is what they add to the already voluminous literature on youth's involvement in drugs and sex. The new dimension is empirical evidence that a personal faith highly predicts a responsible person who evaluates indulgence in light of his goals and their effects on all concerned.

5. A decline on one measure of the cry of joy, namely social action, stands in contrast with the other dimensions. A drop of 3 standard points (from 50 to 47) is significant at a .01 level.

6. The differences in score averages between 1970 and 1985 are quite striking. Most notable is the student "t" of 30.17 for religious participation, followed by 20.64 for self-regard and 19.44 for God awareness. A smaller but significant difference (at .01 level) appears for moral responsibility—10.63. The only dimension (of those for which a measure is available) showing no significant advance is the measure for meaningful life. This suggests that there was no advance over 1970 in the desire of 1985 youth to serve.

7. Reaching Out

1. This write-up summarizing reports from ninety-one effective youth leaders was prepared by Dr. Francis Gamelin, former president of Higher Education Coordinating Council, St. Louis, Missouri. His account, found on pp. 7.9–7.12, is given in "Descriptive Studies of Church Youth Workers," published by Search Institute.

Bibliography

Adelson, J. 1986. *Inventing adolescence: The political psychology of everyday schooling.* New Brunswick, NJ: Transaction Books.

Adorno, T. W., E. Frenkel-Brunswik, D. J. Levinson, and R. N. Sanford. 1950. *The authoritarian personality.* Vol. 1 New York: Harper & Row.

———. 1964. *The authoritarian personality.* Vol. 2. New York: Wiley, Science Editions.

Allen, R. O., and B. Spilka. 1967. Committed and consensual religion: A specification of religion-prejudice relationships. *Journal for the Scientific Study of Religion* 6:191–206.

Allport, G. 1954. *The nature of prejudice.* Cambridge, MA: Addison-Wesley.

Allport, G., and J. M. Ross. 1967. Personal religious orientation and prejudice. *Journal of Personal Social Psychology* 5:432–43.

Apter, A., Bleich, A., Plutchik, R. (1988). Suicide behavior, depression, and conduct disorder in hospitalized adolescents. *Journal of American Academy of Child and Adolescent Psychiatry,* 27, 696–99.

Bachman, Jerald G., Lloyd D. Johnson, and Patrick M. O'Malley. 1988. *Monitoring the future.* Survey Research Center—Institute for Social Research. University of Michigan, 174–76.

Bayer, A. E., L. Kent, and J. E. Dutton. 1972. *Christian Century,* June: 708–13.

Bellah, R., R. Madsen, W. M. Sullivan, A. Swidler, and S. N. Tipton. 1985. *Habits of the heart: Individualism and commitment in American life.* New York: Haprer & Row.

Benson, Peter L. 1990. *The troubled journey: a portrait of 6th–12th grade youth.* Minneapolis: Lutheran Brotherhood.

Benson, P., and B. Spilka. 1972. God image as a function of self-esteem and locus of control. Paper presented at the International Congress of Learned Societies in the Field of Religion, Los Angeles, CA.

Benson, Peter L., and Dorothy L. Williams. 1982. *Religion on capitol hill: myths and realities.* San Francisco: Harper and Row, 157.

Berman, Alan L. and David A. Jobes. 1991. Adolescent suicide: Assessment and intervention. Washington DC: *American Psychological Association.*

Berman, A. L. and R. Schwartz, 1990. Suicide among adolescent drug users. *American Journal of Diseases of Children.* 144, 310–14.

Bernard, J. 1966. Marital stability and patterns of status variables. *Journal of Marriage and the Family* 28:423.

Bettelheim, B. 1969. *The children of the dream.* New York: Macmillan.

Biddy, R. W., and D. C. Posterski. 1985. *The emerging generation: An inside look at Canada's teenagers.* Toronto: Irwin Publishing.

Buehler, C., G. Hesser, and A. Weigert. 1976. A study of articles on religion in major sociology journals. *Journals for the Scientific Study of Religion* 15:15–28.

Campbell, W. D. 1962. *Race and the renewal of the church.* Philadelphia: Westminster Press.

Chapman, R. 1963. *The lonliness of man.* London: SCM Press.

Chipman, D. A., II. 1972. Characteristics of liberal arts college student marijuana users. *Journal of College Student Personnel,* November, 511–17.

Corbett, J. M., and C. E. Johnson. 1972. *It's happening with youth.* New York: Harper & Row.

de Lone, R. H. 1972. The ups and downs of drug-abuse education. *Saturday Review of Education,* November, 27–32.

Dentler, R. A. 1967. *Major social problems.* Chicago: Rand McNally.

Dittes, J. E. 1973. *Bias and the pious.* Minneapolis: Augsburg.

Dizmang, L. H. 1967. Suicide among the Cheyenne Indians. *Bulletin of Suicidology,* July, 8–11.

———. 1970. Indian teenage suicides shock investigators. *Roche Medical Image and Commentary* 6:11–13.

Dryfoos, Joy G. 1989. *Adolescents at risk: prevalence.* New York: Oxford University Press. vi.

Eklin, Carolyn and Eugene Roehlkepartain. 1992. *Source.* Minneapolis: Search Institute. 1–2.

Farberow, N. L. 1989. Preparatory and prior suicidal behavior factors. Report of the Secretary's Task Force on Youth Suicide: Risk factors for youth suicide: 2:34–55. U.S. Government Printing Office (DHHHS Pub. No. ADM 89-1622)

Flannery, E. 1965. *Anguish of the Jews: Twenty-three centuries of anti-Semitism.* New York: Macmillan.

Forde, G. 1972. *Where God meets man: Luther's down-to-earth approach to the gospel.* Minneapolis: Augsburg.

Gallup, G. Jr. and Bezella, R. 1992. PRRC Emerging trends. *The religious life of young Americans.* Princeton: George H. Gallup Institute.

Giroux, T. 1984. *The mood of American youth.* Washington, DC: National Association of Secondary School Principals.

Goldstein, M. J., E. H. Rodnick, L. L. Judd, and E. Gould. 1970. Galvanic skin reactivity among family groups containing disturbed adolescents. *Journal of Abnormal Psychology* 1:57–67.

Gordon, T. 1970. *Parent effectiveness training: the no-lose way to raise children.* New York: Peter H. Wyden.

Gorsuch, R. L. and M. C. Butler. 1976. Initial drug abuse: A review of predisposing social and psychological factors. *Psych. Bull.* 83:120–137.

Grams, A. 1968. *Changes in family life.* St. Louis: Concordia.

Greeley, A. M. 1972. *Unsecular man.* New York: Schocken Books.

Habel, N. 1969. *For mature adults only.* Philadelphia: Fortress Press.

Hadden, J. K. 1969. The private generation. *Psychology Today* 5:32.

Hall, G. S. 1904. *Adolescence.* Vol. 1. New York: Appleton.

Hanssen, C. A., and M. J. Paulson. 1972. Our anti-establishment youth: Revolution or evolution. *Adolescence* 27:393–408.

Harry, J. 1989. Sexual identity issues. *Report of the Secrtary's Task Force on Youth Suicide: Risk factors for youth suicide.* 2:131–142. U.S. Government Printing Office (DHHS Publication No. ADM 89-1622).

Hastings, P. K. and D. R. Hage. 1970. Religious change among college students over two decades. *Social Forces* 1:16–28.

Havighurst, R. J., and B. Keating. 1971. The religion of youth. In *Research on religious development,* edited by M. P. Strommen, pp. 686–723. New York: Hawthorn Books.

Hayes, C. D., ed. 1987. *Risking the future: Adolescent sexuality, pregnancy, and childbearing.* Washington, DC: National Academy Press.

Heath, D. H. 1969. Secularization and maturity of religious beliefs. *Journal of Religion and Health* 4:335–58.

Hines, W. 1972. How 455 in 1,000 marriages break up. *Minneapolis Star,* July 11.

Hodgkinson, H. L. 1986. The patterns of our social fabric are changing. *Education Week,* May 14.

Hodgkinson, H. L. 1986. Here they come, ready or not. *Education Week Special Report,* May 14, p. 22.

Jacobs, J. 1971. *Adolescent suicide.* New York: Wiley.

Johnson, D. W., and G. W. Cornell. 1972. *Punctured preconceptions.* New York: Friendship Press.

Johnston, J., and J. Bachman. 1971. *Young men look at military service: Preliminary report.* Ann Arbor: Survey Research Institute, Institute for Social Research at the University of Michigan.

Josephson, E., and M. Josephson, eds. 1962. *Man alone: Alienation in modern society.* New York: Dell.

Kandel, D. B., and G. S. Lesser. 1972. *Youth in two worlds.* San Francisco: Jossey-Bass.

Kaufman, B. 1972. *Up the down staircase.* New York: Avon.

Keniston, K. 1960. *The uncommitted: Alienated youth in American society.* New York: Harcourt.

Kiell, N. 1964. *The universal experience of adolescents.* New York: International Universities Press.

Klein, D. F. 1972. Youthful rebels—diagnosis and treatment. *Adolescence* 27:351–69.

Kushnick, L. 1987. Race relations in the United States. *Encyclopedia Britannica, Book of the Year.*

Kushnick, Louis. 1992. Race relations. *Britannica.* Book of the Year 1992. Chicago: Encyclopedia Britannica. 258–259.

Larson, D. B., A. R. Omraw, D. G. Blazer, E. M. Pattison, and B. H. Kaplan. 1983. A review of religious research in four major psychiatric journals: 1978–1982. Unpublished paper. National Institute of Mental Health.

Life. 1969. What people think about their high schools: A survey by Louis Harris. May 16.

Lipset, S. M. 1987. Blacks and Jews: How much bias? *Public Opinion.* July/August, 4–5, 57–58.

Little, S. 1968. *Youth, world, and church.* Richmond, VA: John Knox Press.

McCain, T. 1973. Written before I became a Christian. *Focus on youth.* 14 (Winter): 11.

Marty, M. E. 1958. *The new shape of American religion.* New York: Harper & Bros.

———. 1965. *Youth considers "do-it-yourself" religion.* New York: Thomas Nelson.

Mead, M. 1970. *Culture and commitment: A study of the generation gap.* Garden City, NY: Natural History Press.

Merton, R. K., and R. A. Nisbet, eds. 1961. *Contemporary social problems.* New York: Harcourt, Brace & World.

Minneapolis Star, June 22, 1972. Alcoholism growing as a teen-age problem.

Minneapolis Tribune, August 6, 1972. Loneliness, doubt led comedian's son into drug addiction.

Mirthes, C. 1971. *Can't you hear me talking to you?* New York: Bantam Books.

Morris, J. 1965. *Marriage counseling.* Englewood Cliffs, NJ: Prentice-Hall.

Muuss, R. E. 1962. *Theories of adolescence.* New York: Random House.

National Academy of Sciences. 1984. *Bereavement.* Washington, DC: National Academy Press.

National Association of Secondary Schools. 1984. *The mood of American youth.* 1904. Association Drive, Reston, VA.

National Catholic Educational Association. 1986. *Catholic high schools: Their impact on low-income students.* Washington, DC.

———. 1985. *The Catholic high school: A national portrait.* Washington, DC.

Offer, D., E. Astrov, and K. I. Howard. 1981. *The adolescent: A psychological portrait.* New York: Basic Books.

Opter, A., A. Bleich, R. Plutchik, S. Mendelsohn, and S. Tyano. 1988. Suicidal behavior, depression, and conduct disorder in hospitalized adolescents. *Journal of the American Academy of Child and Adolescent Psychiatry.* 27, 696–699.

Oxford Analytica. 1986. *America in perspective.* Boston: Houghton Mifflin Company.

Pedersen, P. 1968. Religion as a basis of social change among the Bataks of North Sumatra. Ph.D. diss., Claremont Graduate School.

Pfeffer, C. R. 1989. Family characteristics and support systems as risk factors for youth suicide. *Report of the Secretary's Task Force on Youth Suicide: Risk factors for youth suicide.* 2:71–81. U.S. Government Printing Office (DHHS Pub. No. ADM 89-1622).

Posterski, D. C. 1985. *Friendship.* Scarborough, Canada: Project Teen Canada.

Princeton Religion Research Center. 1986. *Faith development and your ministry.* Report based on a Gallup survey conducted for the Religious Education Association, Princeton, NJ.

Randers, J., and D. H. Meadows. 1972. The carrying capacity of the globe. *Sloan management review* 2:11–27.

Reich, C. A. 1970. *The greening of America.* New York: Random House.

Rich, C. L., D. Young, and E. C. Fowler. 1986. San Diego suicide study 1: Young vs. old subjects. *Archives of General Psychiatry.* 43, 577–582.

Rogers, J. M. 1971. Drug abuse, just what the doctor ordered. *Psychology Today* 5:24.

Rokeach, M. 1960. *The open and closed mind.* New York: Basic Books.

Rosenberg, M. 1965. *Society and the adolescent self-image.* Princeton: Princeton University Press.

Sabine, G. 1971. *When you listen, this is what you can hear.* Iowa City, IA: ACT Publications.

Sebald, H. 1968. *Adolescence: A sociological analysis.* New York: Appleton-Century-Crofts.

———. 1972. The pursuit of "instantness" in technocratic society and youth's psychedelic drug use. *Adolescence* 27:343–50.

Seiden, R. H. 1966. Campus tragedy: A study of student suicide. *Journal of Abnormal Psychology* 6:389–99.

———. 1969. Suicide among youth: A report prepared for the Joint Commission on Mental Health of Children. A supplement to the *Bulletin of Suicidology.* Washington, DC: U.S. Government Printing Office.

Shannon, Bishop J. P. 1972. The pilgrim church. *Minneapolis Tribune,* November 12.

Shneidman, E. 1985. *Definition of suicide.* New York: John Wiley & Sons.

Sorenson, R. C. 1973. *Adolescent sexuality in contemporary America.* New York: World.

Spilka, B., R. W. Hood Jr., and R. L. Gorsuch. 1985. *Psychology of religion: An empirical approach.* Englewood Cliffs, NJ: Prentice-Hall.

Stack, S. 1983. The effect of the decline in institutionalized religion on suicide, 1954–1978. *Journal for the Scientific Study of Religion* 22:239–52.

———. 1984. A leveling off in young suicides. *Wall Street Journal,* May 28.

———. 1986. Suggestion and suicide. Paper presented at American Sociological Association. Washington, DC: Family Research Council.

Strommen, M. P. 1963. *Profiles of church youth*. St. Louis: Concordia.

———. 1973. *Bridging the gap*. Minneapolis: Augsburg.

———. 1982. Five Cries of Lutheran parochial school students. *Lutheran Sunday Schools Quarterly*.

Strommen, M. P., and R. K. Gupta. 1971. *Manual for youth research survey: Section 4*. Minneapolis: Youth Research Center.

Strommen, M. P., M. L. Brekke, R. C. Underwager, and A. L. Johnson. 1972. *A study of generations*. Minneapolis: Augsburg.

Strommen, M. P., and A. I. Strommen. 1985. *Five cries of parents*. San Francisco: Harper & Row.

The United Presbyterian Church in the U.S.A. 1970. *The world of church youth: A study of United Presbyterian youth and their leaders, parents and pastors*. Philadelphia: Board of Christian Education.

Time. 1972. Teen-age sex: Letting the pendulum swing. August 21, p. 34.

Turner, J., et al. 1984. *The Ku Klux Klan: A history of racism and violence*. Montgomery, AL: Klanwatch.

U.S. Department of Education. 1986. *What works*. Washington, DC: U.S. Government Printing Office.

U.S. News and World Report. 1971. End of the "youth revolt"?: Survey of changing mood. August 9, pp. 26–31.

Varenhorst, B. 1983. *Real friends: Becoming the friend you'd like to have*. San Francisco: Harper & Row.

Who's Who Among American High School Students. 1972. Results of annual survey reported in *Youth Today*.

Williams, D., ed. 1987. *Yes You Can!* Minneapolis: Search Institute.

Woodyard, D. O. 1969. *To be human now*. Philadelphia: Westminster Press.

Wrenn, C. G. 1973. *The world of the contemporary counselor*. Boston: Houghton Mifflin.

Yankelovich, D. 1969. What they believe: A *Fortune* survey. In *Youth in Turmoil*. New York: Time-Life.

Youth Update. 1992. Minneapolis: *Search Institue*, May, p. 1.

Zinsmeister, K. 1987. Asians: Prejudice from top and bottom. *Public Opinion*, July/August, 8-10, 59.